Asperger's and You

A self-exploration workbook for teens and young adults on the autism spectrum

Acknowledgements

With thanks to Noushka Galley for her illustrations. Noushka is an illustrator and is on the autism spectrum. Visit her website at http://noushka7.wixsite.com/autism

Asperger's and You

A self-exploration workbook for teens and young adults on the autism spectrum

Victoria Honeybourne

First published in 2018 by Crooked Steeple Publishing, Cleobury Mortimer, UK.

ISBN: 978-0-9957810-3-0

Contents

Introduction

Welcome to 'Asperger's and You: A self-exploration workbook for teens and young adults on the autism spectrum'. This book has been designed mainly for teenagers and young adults between the ages of 14 and 30, though older adults might also find parts of the book useful.

There are six sections and some might be more relevant to you than others. You do not have to use the whole book and you do not have to do all of the activities. You can work through the book in any order, take as long as you want, and there are no right or wrong answers! You do not even have to show your answers to anybody, unless you would find it useful.

This book has been designed to help you make sense of who you are. You will learn more about yourself, your Asperger's (or other autism spectrum condition), and how you interact with the world. There are pages for you to read but there are also activities to do, ideas to put into practice and issues to think about. The more you are willing to put in, the more you will get out of this book.

The first edition of this book, 'Your Autism Journey: A self-exploration workbook for young women on the autism spectrum', was aimed predominantly at females, due to some of the specific challenges they face. Feedback suggested that much of the content would be just as useful to males, so this second edition reflects that demand.

The underlying principles, however, remain the same. The book aims to help you to understand yourself, to increase your confidence and to develop practical skills to make the most of situations and events. The aim is not to make you 'less autistic', but to help you to be happier being yourself.

Self

Section 1: Self

This first section is all about you! You will learn more about:

- Who you are
- Your likes and dislikes
- Your strengths, skills and talents
- Self-esteem and confidence
- Sensory sensitivities
- Your Asperger's (Autism)

Let's begin by telling you more about this book. There are pages for you to read and there are questions for you to think about. There are also links to reliable websites and other books where you can find more information about the topics covered.

You may like to have a separate notebook, journal or computer file to make notes in as you go along. Remember there is no 'right' way of doing things; you might like to write, draw, make a collage, type, or even paint. You might write a few pages or just a few words. You might leave some activities out, or come back to them at a later date. This is your journey so it is totally up to you.

Let's get started! The first activities are all about you: your likes, strengths and talents. Let's find out what makes you 'you'!

Activity

What are your favourite things? You could make a list, spider diagram, drawing or collage in your notebook.

Your favourite...

Colour?	*Animal?*
TV Show?	*Book?*
Food?	*Drink?*
Item of Clothing?	*Place?*

Some of your favourite things, likes and dislikes might change over time; others might stay the same. You might add to your lists or drawings as time goes on. These initial activities are designed to help you to start to consider what is important to you and what makes you unique.

Activity

What about your likes and dislikes? Try writing, drawing or thinking about some of the following...

I like to eat ……… . and I don't like to eat ………

I like to watch ……… and I don't like to watch ………

With friends I like to ……… and I don't like to ………

I like to wear ……… and I don't like to wear ………

In school / college I like ……… and I don't like ………

I like people who …… and I don't like people who ………

At the weekend I like to … … and I don't like to … … …

Perhaps you add other sentences of your own.

Your lists will be unique. No two people are exactly the same - even individuals who are all on the autism spectrum are all very different from one another. Let's look now a little more about what it means to be on the autism spectrum.

All about autism

You are probably reading this because you have been told you have Asperger Syndrome, which is an autism spectrum condition. You might have received a diagnosis of 'Autism Spectrum Disorder' or 'High Functioning Autism'.

Being 'on the autism spectrum' means that you connect, communicate and interact with others in a different way. You might not be particularly interested in other people, or you might find it difficult to make friends, even when you try very hard. Perhaps you find it difficult to understand other people, or they seem to find it difficult to understand you.

Being on the autism spectrum means you interpret the world differently than people who are not autistic. Perhaps you feel that your logic and reasoning is not shared by others, or maybe you notice things that others do not. You might also experience different reactions to various sensory inputs such as lights, noise, touch and textures. In general, you probably find people and the world confusing, unpredictable and, at times, overwhelming! Sometimes being autistic has been described as feeling a bit like an alien in a world full of humans; it can seem like everybody else has been given the rulebook and you have not.

Autism spectrum conditions are considered to be 'neurodevelopmental differences'. This means that they are something that you are born with and affect you throughout your life. Nobody yet knows exactly why they occur, but they are more common than people believe.

Sometimes you will see autism described as a disability or a disorder, but most people nowadays realise that autism is just a different way of being. They believe many difficulties are caused mainly because other people are not yet tolerant or accepting enough of these differences. They propose the world has been designed only for 'neurotypical' people, sometimes putting others at a disadvantage.

You will learn more about being on the autism spectrum throughout this book. Autism is considered a spectrum, meaning you might share some similarities with others on the autism spectrum, but not necessarily. Each individual has different strengths, talents, likes, abilities and experiences, and will react to and experience their autism differently.

Being on the autism spectrum can make life seem difficult at times! Sometimes it is easy to think that life would perhaps be easier if you were not on the autism spectrum. That is ok; everybody has times when they would prefer to be somebody else! However, autism is really not a negative. Being on the autism spectrum does not stop you doing well at college or university, getting a job that you enjoy, or being happy. Many people on the autism spectrum are very successful and have learned how to make the most of their individual strengths and interests.

Activity

What are your initial thoughts about being on the autism spectrum? Are they generally positive or negative? Do you have any concerns?

Your diagnosis of an autism spectrum condition might have been a positive and reassuring explanation for why you have always felt different. It might have helped you to understand and accept some of your differences.

The rest of this book will support you to learn more about yourself and your autism. You will learn how to improve your self-esteem and confidence and find out how to identify what is meaningful to you. You will also learn how to communicate more effectively with others, how to get on in education and employment, and how to cope with various problems that come up in life. This book cannot, however, cover everything and there are also plenty of links to further information and support.

More about you

What are your hobbies and interests? We all have things we enjoy doing and topics that we are passionate about. Perhaps you enjoy crafting, drawing, painting, playing a musical instrument, listening to music, abseiling, watching films, playing sports, walking the dog, reading, sewing, making things, using the computer, gardening, baking, dancing or martial arts? Perhaps there are topics and causes that you feel particularly strongly about: the environment, animal welfare, volunteering, helping the elderly, human rights, promoting awareness for a charity or cause, removing injustice? Or perhaps you have a specific interest that you are very knowledgeable about: a historical period, a foreign country, a sport or activity, a book, computers, wildlife, animals?

Spending time doing things you enjoy or that are important to you can help you to feel happy, relaxed and purposeful. Try to spend some time each week doing things you enjoy. You could see if there are any clubs or groups in your school / college / university / local area which cater for your interests. This can be a good way of getting to know people with similar interests and values.

Special interests

Sometimes, individuals on the autism spectrum have what is known as a 'special interest'. This just means that there is an interest which you feel particularly intensely and strongly about; the interest may dominate your life and you might find it hard to concentrate on anything else. You might be very knowledgeable about the interest and find out everything you can about it. This interest may be the only thing you want to talk about or the only thing you want to do.

Having a special interest can be great – indeed, many people become experts in their field and go on to study or work in a job related to their interest. Their in-depth knowledge and focus can be a real advantage.

Having a special interest can also be very pleasurable and enjoyable. Have you ever been so absorbed in your interest that you lost track of time and did not notice what was happening around you? If so, you have experienced what psychologists call 'flow': the enjoyable experience of being totally engaged in what you are doing.[iii] Experiencing this is known to be beneficial to happiness levels and wellbeing.

Having interests is great. Occasionally, however, an interest might begin to have a negative impact on the rest of your life, because it takes up all of your time and thoughts.

If this applies to you, try to become aware of things you might be neglecting to do. You could try simply making a list of the important things that you need to do (e.g. taking a shower, eating breakfast, jobs in the house, work, homework) and make sure you do those things first. Then you can enjoy spending the rest of your time on your hobby or interest without having to worry that you have forgotten to do something important. This also removes the need for other people to interrupt you (or nag you!) about doing things.

Another strategy could be to schedule a set time to work on your interest in your weekly planner or timetable. Alternatively, you might like to set an alarm so that you know when it is time to switch to another task. Try a few things and see what works best for you. Be aware too, that not everybody else might share your knowledge and interest in a subject. It can be boring to listen to somebody talk continuously about something you are not interested in, so try to monitor yourself and your topics of conversation. If you have been talking for too long, change the subject or ask the listener about something they are interested in.

Let's look now at what you do well. This will help you identify the skills and strengths you possess.

Activity

What have you done well in the past? Make a list in your journal or notepad of your achievements. Achievements can be big or small. They can be anything you have worked hard at, improved at, done well, or tried for the first time.

Here are some examples:

I was scared of water but persevered and learned how to swim.

I went along to an aerobics class, even though I was worried about going by myself.

I put a lot of time into revising for my Maths exam.

I asked for help when I needed it in my first week at university.

Maybe you found it difficult to list your achievements? That is ok. Sometimes it can be hard to recognise or remember all of the things we have done well. Try the next activity to help you to add to your achievement list.

Activity

In your journal or notepad, try to note down at least two or three things that go well each day. These things can be big or small. Try to do this every day for a week, or month. You might even like to carry it on after that.

Example:

> **Monday**
>
> *I started a conversation with a new student at college.*
>
> *I walked the dog and enjoyed being outside in the fresh air.*

We've looked at your likes, dislikes, interests and achievements. Now let's investigate your characteristics, strengths and values.

Activity

Which words would you use to describe yourself? Make a list or spider diagram in your journal or notepad. Perhaps you could draw a picture of yourself or stick a photo in the centre. There is a list of useful words below which you might like to choose from or add your own.

Why have you chosen these words to describe yourself? Can you think of evidence for each word you have chosen?

Possible words to describe yourself

Quiet	Loud	Shy
Generous	Funny	Friendly
Kind	Lazy	Hard-working
Introverted	Extroverted	Sociable
Intelligent	Thoughtful	Polite
Lively	Energetic	Enthusiastic
Considerate	Musical	Sporty
Creative	Arty	Innovative
Talkative	Nervous	Anxious
Curious	Different	Unique
Boring	Interested	Helpful
Determined	Curious	Independent

Activity

Sometimes other people can influence how we see ourselves. Have other people ever told you what sort of person they think you are? Maybe you could make a list of words that other people have used to describe you.

Take a look at your list. Remember, just because somebody says something or believes something, does not mean it is true! It is simply their personal opinion, and they might be deliberately trying to be unkind.

Try completing these sentences:

Some people think I am .... but I know that I am ....

I've been told I am ... ... but I know I am ... ...

The words we use to describe ourselves change over time. As we have more life experiences, learn new things and meet new people, our outlook on life and how we react to situations changes.

Let's turn now to your skills, strengths and values.

Activity

What skills do you have? Make a list, drawing or spider diagram to remind yourself.

A skill is something that you have learned how to do. Some examples might be:

> *Knowing how to play chess.*
>
> *Being able to use specific computer programs.*
>
> *Being able to play a musical instrument.*
>
> *Knowing how to bake a cake.*
>
> *Being able to start a conversation.*

Think about the skills you may have developed through education, employment, volunteering, your hobbies and in your spare time. Keep adding to your list as you acquire new skills. We are constantly learning and improving skills throughout our lives.

Identifying strengths

Identifying your strengths can help you to discover what sort of a person you are, what comes more naturally to you, and what you find more difficult. This knowledge can be especially helpful when you are considering which sort of job or college course you might be best suited for. It can also help you to make more effective decisions in other aspects of your life.

You may like to come back to some of these activities when you have worked through the rest of this book, or at another point in the future. It can become easier to identify your skills and strengths over time, when you have more experiences to reflect on.

Activity

What are your strengths? Strengths go beyond words that you would use to describe your personality. When you use your character strengths you are likely to feel energized, excited, motivated and passionate[vi]; these are things that come most naturally to you. Think whether any of the strengths below describe you. You could ask trusted friends or family members what they think your strengths are. Can they give you evidence to back up what they say?

Creativity	Curiosity
Judgement	Love of learning
Perspective	Bravery
Perseverance	Honesty
Zest	Love
Kindness	Social intelligence
Teamwork	Fairness
Leadership	Forgiveness
Humility	Carefulness
Self-regulation	Awe / Wonder
Gratitude	Hope
Humour	Spirituality

This list of strengths is taken from the VIA Institute on Character (www.viacharacter.org). If you are interested, there is a free online survey which you can take to help you identify your

---

strengths; there is also a youth version designed specifically for 10 – 17 year olds.

It is useful for everybody to become better able to identify their strengths, skills and values, and there are several activities on the topic included in this book as it can be particularly important for individuals on the autism spectrum. Some autistic individuals report that they find it difficult to build a sense of 'self-identity',[vii] perhaps feeling they spend a lot of time trying to fit in with the people around them, and so losing sight of their uniqueness and what is important to them as an individual. The activities in this chapter will help you to identify what is important to you, not just what is important to other people.

Activity

Let's ow consider which values are important to you. A value is something important to you across different contexts. You feel best when you are acting in line with your values. Some ideas are given below. You might like to create a list or spider diagram in your journal. Here are some ideas:

Curiosity	Accomplishment	Calmness
Carefulness	Achievement	Adventure
Challenge	Determination	Cheerfulness
Ambition	Hard work	Art
Education	Awe	Belonging
Energy	Encouragement	Enjoyment
Courage	Creativity	Environment
Hopefulness	Modesty	Expertise
Imagination	Humour	Nature
Individuality	Open-mindedness	Family
Fashion	Fairness	Integrity
Patience	Independence	Forgiveness
Friendship	Kindness	Knowledge
Fun	Generosity	Freedom
Logic	Helpfulness	Truth
Making a difference	Religion	Volunteering
Wisdom	Success	Respect

Plenty more words could be added to this list. Are any other values important to you?

If you find it difficult to identify your values, you could try thinking of somebody (real or fictional, famous or not) who you admire. What are the values in that person that you admire?

You could also try thinking back to a day that you particularly enjoyed or a time when you felt you reacted really well to a situation. Why were you happy or pleased? What were you doing that was important to you?

More about being on the autism spectrum

You might have only just recognised that you are on the autism spectrum, or it might be something you have known about since you were younger. You might feel you already know a lot about autism, or that you know nothing at all! Individuals on the autism spectrum have a range of experiences. Here are just a few things other have said:

I realised I needed something different to other people but didn't want to appear any more different.

I never understood other people and they didn't understand me!

People told me that I was odd and strange.

16

I was desperate to make friends but never seemed to be able to.

I just wanted to be by myself; I wasn't interested in others.

I felt invisible and as if nobody took my perspective seriously.

I tried for a long time to hide my Asperger's. I tried to fit in with people but just ended up more miserable.

I had teachers and friends who were there for me which really helped.

Activity

What about you? What have been your experiences so far? Everybody on the autism spectrum will have different experiences.

In this chapter you might have come across words to describe values, strengths or characteristics which you do not fully understand or have not encountered before. Look them up in a dictionary, online or ask somebody what they mean. This is one small way of beginning a good habit: that of becoming life curious.

Become life curious!

Life can be confusing, complicated and frustrating at times. It can also be amazingly exciting! Becoming 'life curious' helps you to get the most out of life. Look up new words and concepts that you come across, ask about things that you do not understand, try out new activities, visit new places, read about things that are new to you, learn new things, and notice the environment around you. It does not matter if you try something new and do not like it; just being willing to try it out and learning from the process is what's important. By becoming curious about the world around you, you will better be able to identify new possibilities and opportunities.

Interesting Fact

Hans Asperger, who was one of the first doctors to identify autism spectrum conditions (and gave his name to 'Asperger Syndrome') said:

'Not everything that steps out of line, and is thus considered 'abnormal', is necessarily inferior'.

Being on the autism spectrum is merely a difference, it does not make you any less important than anybody else. Indeed, life would be very boring if everybody was exactly the same!

Self-acceptance

If you read about, or listen to, adults on the autism spectrum talking about how they have become successful, you will find most of them identify that gaining 'self-acceptance' was a major turning point. Many discover their self-esteem, happiness and wellbeing all improve when they stop trying to be somebody else, and instead begin to accept and make the most of their autism and own unique way of experiencing the world.

Further information

If you would like to find out more about autism spectrum conditions then a good place to start is the National Autistic Society website (www.autism.org). There is lots of easy-to-read information and advice about autism. The National Autistic

---

Society is based in the UK. If you live elsewhere, you might find that your country has a similar organisation.

Many local geographical areas also have autism organisations which provide advice and support to individuals living in the area, such as 'Autism West Midlands' and 'Scottish Autism'.

Self-esteem

Self-esteem is perhaps best described as what you think about yourself, your level of self-worth or self-respect. People who have a good level of self-esteem are assertive, respect themselves and others, and feel 'happy in their own skin'. People with low self-esteem might not like themselves or be very critical of themselves. They might find it difficult to be assertive and to set helpful boundaries. They might feel unable to make decisions, might believe that nobody likes them, and might be low in confidence.

Having low self-esteem can be a common difficulty which can have a negative impact on many aspects of life. Sometimes, individuals on the autism spectrum may have particular reasons for developing low self-esteem[viii]: perhaps they have been told by others that they are 'different', 'odd' or 'not good enough', or perhaps they find they often compare themselves to others.

Activity

If you feel you have low self-esteem, perhaps you could write about this in your journal. Think about what could be affecting your self-esteem and consider if there have been times when you thought more positively about yourself. Remember your levels of self-esteem are not fixed and you can learn how to improve this. Some useful strategies are outlined in later chapters of this book.

You might also benefit from talking about your concerns with a counsellor or therapist – there is more information later in this chapter. If you like to find information independently, there is also information about self-esteem on the Young Minds website (www.youngminds.org.uk), the Mind website (www.mind.org.uk) and the NHS website (www.nhs.uk).

Confidence

Self-confidence simply means having confidence in yourself. Confidence grows out of self-esteem, feelings of well-being, and a belief in your own abilities and skills. Confidence levels can vary from day to day and from situation to situation. When you are not feeling confident, you might be afraid of making mistakes and may not believe that you can do something. These feelings can stop you from taking part in activities and events that you might enjoy.

Activity

Make some notes in your journal. When do you feel most confident? When do you feel less confident? Why is this? Is there anything that you avoid doing because you do not feel confident enough?

The good news is that there are lots of things that you can do to help you feel more confident.

Interesting Fact

Many people avoid doing things because they do not feel confident enough. They want to wait until they feel more confident. It is actually only through doing things and 'having a go', however, that we develop confidence! Confidence develops through experience, preparation, learning from mistakes and a positive attitude. Avoiding things does not make you any more confident about them in the future; sometimes the only way to develop confidence is to do the scary thing!

Developing confidence

One possible strategy to develop confidence for a situation can be to think about the best and worst case scenario. Let's look at an example:

Imagine you have to give a presentation to a large group of people. Consider first the best case scenario. If everything went perfectly, what would happen? Perhaps you included some of these ideas: you would feel confident and well-prepared; you would look forward to the event; you would create a clear and well-structured presentation; you would stand confidently and speak loudly and clearly; you would remember everything you wanted to say and you would enjoy yourself when talking. Perhaps you would even make some jokes! The audience would look interested and enthusiastic and they would ask lots of interesting questions afterwards. You would be able to give informative answers.

Next, consider the worst case scenario. What could be the absolute worst that could happen? Perhaps you would be so nervous you would turn bright red, your mouth would go dry and you wouldn't be able to speak loudly enough? Maybe you would forget everything you wanted to say? Perhaps the audience would not be interested in what you were saying? Maybe you would trip over in front of everybody, or your trousers would suddenly and inexplicably fall down? Perhaps nobody would clap or ask any questions?

In reality, the actual event is always likely to be somewhere between these two extremes. Sometimes, considering the 'worst case scenario' can help us to realise that actually the worst that can happen is not actually all that bad. For example, you might not feel confident enough to apply for a part-time job that you have seen advertised. What is the absolute worst that can happen? You send the application but do not hear back and are not successful in getting an interview. That's actually not so bad when you consider it. In that case the worst that can happen is – nothing!

Thinking about the worst case scenario can also help you to plan and prepare for the scary event. So, in the example of giving a presentation you could write out some notes about what you wanted to say; this would ensure that, if you did forget anything, you could look at your notes and read from them. You could also practise your presentation in advance and perhaps film yourself when practising to watch it back and see how to improve it. You could make sure you wore something comfortable to avoid any potentially embarrassing wardrobe malfunction, and could take a bottle of water to drink if your mouth goes dry with nerves.

Activity

There are several things you can do to help you to feel more confident. You might like to try the 'best and worst case' scenario thinking outlined above. You might feel more confident if you have planned and prepared for the new situation – think about what you might find difficult and how you could overcome this. Taking some time to research and learn about an event can also improve confidence levels beforehand.

When you have tried something new, reflect on what went well and consider how you could learn from the aspects that did not go so well. You might like to discuss these with another person, or reflect on these in your journal.

Sensory sensitivities

Humans have five main senses: those of sight, sound, smell, touch and texture. Everybody, not just those on the autism spectrum, has different sensory preferences and tolerances.

We all have sensory likes and dislikes. Some of these dislikes might even be quite intense; plenty of people hate sprouts, for example, or find the smell of sweaty shoes particularly putrid! Different people also have different sensory tolerances. Some people like to listen to very loud music, for example, while others prefer a lower of music or television.

Activity

What are your sensory likes and dislikes? Try making lists, spider diagrams or charts of sensory input that you like (sights, sounds, smells, textures and tastes) and ones you dislike.

Some people on the autism spectrum experience specific sensory sensitivities. This is when sensory input is so intense it feels incredibly uncomfortable or even painful. This is called 'hyper-sensitivity' (or over-sensitivity). Others on the autism spectrum can be under-sensitive ('hypo-sensitive') to sensory input; they can be completely oblivious to smells, for example, or might not be sensitive to taste. Under-sensitivity can have downsides – the individual might not recognise when they have body odour, or might eat non-food items because they are the only things that taste good.

If you experience sensory sensitivities there are many strategies you can try or adapt to make things easier. Here are some ideas:

- Cut labels out of clothing if you are irritated by them
- Choose clothing in soft fabrics that you find comfortable
- Wear ear plugs or headphones in noisy environments to block out the sound
- Wear glasses with tinted lenses if you find bright lights uncomfortable
- Find a quiet place to study or to relax in if you find it difficult to block out background noise
- Limit time in places you find overwhelming to your senses (e.g. busy, noisy, brightly-lit shopping centres). Visit them at quieter times or find an alternative such as a local shop or ordering online
- Keep your workspace, room or house neat and tidy if you are overwhelmed by too many distractions in your environment

- Experiment with different lighting at home until you find the most comfortable levels
- Arrange to meet friends in quieter places if you find it easier to follow a conversation when there is less background noise
- If you share a house or office, tell your housemates or colleagues about any sensory issues which cause you particular distress so that they are aware of this

---

Activity

If you experience particular sensory sensitivities, make a note of these. What could you do to help you to cope with these, or to minimise your discomfort?

Some individuals on the autism spectrum find some sensory input so overwhelming that it can cause them a lot of distress. They can find it impossible to block out the input and can become unable to concentrate or communicate. It can become impossible to focus on what is going on when in this state of anxiety and some individuals may shutdown or meltdown completely.

If this applies to you, consider what the triggers are. You might be able to identify how you could avoid, or cope with, some of these things. Experiment and learn what helps you to recover from overwhelming sensory input. It might be, for example, that you need some time completely alone in a quiet space away from any sensory input or people to recover. Explore the things that work for you in your journal.

Many people on the autism spectrum learn how to cope very effectively with their sensory sensitivities. Raising awareness amongst your family, friends and tutors can help, as can developing a bank of successful coping strategies. You might also become less sensitive to some things over time. Often tolerance levels to sensory input fluctuate according to our anxiety levels.

Although we have five main senses, there are also other 'senses', such as balance, spatial awareness, and body awareness. These are further areas that some individuals on the autism spectrum may find difficult. Some can find it difficult to judge an appropriate distance between themselves and other people, or need more personal space than other people. Others might appear to be very clumsy or often bump into things. If this applies to you, consider what you could do to help. Simply moving furniture to the outside of the room might stop you from tripping over it.

Interesting Fact

People who volunteer their time to others are often happier than those who do not. Volunteering also enables you to meet new people, learn new skills and make a difference. Do any of the following appeal to you?

Donating blood? Fundraising for a charity? Raising awareness for a cause? Helping the elderly? Supporting somebody who is disabled or disadvantaged? Caring for animals who have been neglected? Volunteering with children? Volunteering on an environmental project?

Opportunities might be displayed in your student services centre or local community. Alternatively, look on websites such as www.ncvo.org.uk (The National Council for Voluntary Organisations) or do-it.org

---

Routine and structure

We all, whether on the autism spectrum or not, like to have some routines and structures in our lives. Many of us, for example, do the same things in the same order every morning before we go out; this can be a predictable routine which ensures we remember to do everything we need to. It can be unsettling when this routine is broken as we are thrown out of our comfort zone and have to do things differently; this often involves us having to come out of 'autopilot' and think about things in more detail. It is an uneasy feeling as our brain has to get used to something new.

Having a familiar routine and structure is necessary for all of us; it helps us to feel more comfortable and reduces anxiety. Individuals on the autism spectrum often have a greater reliance on routine, structure and predictability than others. It makes sense that if we find the world or other people confusing and unpredictable, having set routines in place can reduce our anxieties by making the day seem more predictable.

Activity

What about you? Do you have certain routines and structures in place which you like to follow at home, school, college or work? What are these?

How do you feel if you cannot follow your routine? Are there any times when having a set routine has been unhelpful?

There will always be times when things do not go 'to plan'. There are times when circumstances outside our control mean that we have to do things differently. Having a 'Plan B' can help to reduce worry and anxiety. Consider what you will do if something does not go to plan. For example, if your train was cancelled, what would you alternative be?

Getting Support

This section of the book has been all about you. You have had chance to consider who you are; your likes and dislikes; your strengths, skills and values; your self-esteem and confidence; and your sensory needs. You have also begun to find out a little more about autism and how it affects you. Come back to these activities as often as you need to, as your understanding of yourself develops.

Further information

Some people find it helpful to read about others who are on the autism spectrum.

'Freaks, Geeks and Asperger Syndrome' is a book by Luke Jackson is one such example. 'M is for Autism' (Jessica Kingsley Publishers, 2015) is a novel written by the students at Limpsfield Grange, a school for girls on the autism spectrum. More autobiographical accounts from females on the autism spectrum include 'Pretending to be Normal' by Liane Holliday-Wiley, 'Martian in the Playground' by Claire Sainsbury, 'Women and Girls with Autism Spectrum Disorder' by Sarah Hendrickx, 'Women from Another Planet' by Jean Kearns-Miller and 'Ultraviolet Voices: Stories of Women on the Autism Spectrum' published by Autism West Midlands. 'The Girl with the Curly Hair' books also cover various aspects of Asperger's.

There are plenty more books available which look at specific aspects of life on the autism spectrum (e.g. employment, university life, staying safe, school). You may be able to find these in your local library or bookstore.

You will learn more reading this book, but it is also useful to know where you can get more support. This book does not cover everything and there may be some areas you would like more in-depth help with. Who could you talk to?

Parents, relatives and friends

You may have trusted family members, relatives or friends who you can discuss things with. This can be useful as they know you well and often want to help when they can. However, sometimes there are things you might prefer to discuss with a professional outside your immediate environment, or with somebody who has specific knowledge or expertise.

Teachers and tutors

Teachers, tutors and learning support assistants in your school, college or university can help you with academic-related issues. If you are having difficulty with learning and studying, or with completing an assignment, these are the people to talk to. You might be able to speak to them face-to-face or email them to make an appointment for when you can speak to them. There are also tips about studying in the 'Learning' section of this book.

Mentors

A mentor is generally somebody who is more experienced than you in a particular field. They give you advice and guidance. Some people have a workplace mentor; this is usually somebody who has been doing the job for a while and helps you to learn what to do and to improve at your job. Sometimes school and college students have 'peer mentors'; these are (usually) students who are slightly older than you who can help you to settle in and can help you to solve any problems that you might have related to the new environment. Some colleges, universities and workplaces also offer specialist autism mentors; this will be somebody with experience of autism who can support you to overcome any difficulties that you may face.

Counsellors and therapists

Counsellors and therapists are professionals you can talk to about your thoughts and feelings. They can help you to explore how you feel, and can help you cope with issues such as grief, depression and anxiety. They have specific qualifications and are very experienced. They use a range of different therapies to help you make sense of your thoughts, feelings and behaviour; some involve talking, while others may involve art, music, drama or play. If you are at school, college or university, then your institution should offer a student counselling service. Usually you can ask to be referred to them, attend a drop-in session, or email to make an appointment. If you have finished your education, or if your establishment does not offer a counselling service, then you can often self-refer or be referred to a therapist through your doctor (GP). Make an appointment with them, tell them what is concerning you, and ask to be referred.

Doctors, nurses and other health professionals

If you are concerned about an aspect of your physical health, then it is best to speak to a doctor, nurse or other health professional. You may have a physical illness, physical symptoms, or be concerned about puberty or your sexual health. Again, most schools, college and universities have a nurse who can offer drop-in sessions or appointments. Alternatively, visit your doctor who can advise on the services that will be most suitable.

Speech and language therapists

Speech and language therapists work with individuals and groups on their speech, language and communication skills. They can help you to develop your social communication skills and conversational skills. Your school or college may offer you some sessions with a speech and language therapist. There are also some ideas about improving communication skills in Section 3 of this book.

Careers' advisors

If you want to discuss your future career options, careers advisors are experienced in supporting young people to consider various options and make decisions. Your school, college or university will offer a careers service; you should be able to make an appointment to speak to somebody. If you have left education and are looking for a job; then you should speak to an advisor at your local job centre. There is more information in the 'Employment' section of this book.

Social workers and family support workers

Social workers and family support workers help families or individuals who are experiencing times of difficulty. You might have a social worker, for example, if you have been taken into foster care or are looked after by somebody other than your parents. Social workers and family support workers can help you to make sense of these situations and to deal with practical aspects too.

More about autism

As you read and listen to more about the autism spectrum you will hear different terminology used and will realise that different people approach the topic from different perspectives.

The Medical Model. The medical model of disability proposes that difficulties are within the individual affected. Its aim is to 'fix', 'cure' or 'treat' the individual to make them more 'typical', often through medication or therapy.

The Social Model. This model proposes that difficulties for individuals are created by the society in which they live. Society have been designed for just one way of being and those who do not fit this profile are placed at a disadvantage.

Neurodiversity. The term neurodiversity simply means that there is a range of ways in which human brains think, learn and relate to others. These differences are a normal and natural aspect of human variation to be expected and accepted. No one way of being is superior to any other.

What about you? What are your thoughts? Do you agree or disagree with any of the positions outlined above? It is ok not to be sure what you think.

The next sections of this book look at health and wellbeing; friendships, relationships and communication; learning; employment; and life skills. You will continue to learn more about yourself and your autism, and to add to your journal or notebook.

Activity

Reflect on what you have learned so far in your journal. What have you discovered about yourself and what is important to you? Which strategies are you going to test out and what are you going to find out more about? How will you do this?

Your favourite words…

Inspirational quotes…

Scribble Page…

What inspires you…

A fictional character
you would like to have
as a friend…

Health & Wellbeing

Section 2: Health & Wellbeing

This section covers issues such as physical health, body image, puberty and mental wellbeing.

Physical Wellbeing

Let's begin by considering physical wellbeing. Physical wellbeing means supporting our bodies to function as well as they can. This improves our physical health and fitness and also has a positive impact on our mental and emotional wellbeing too.

Sleep

How do you feel if you have not slept very well? A lack of sleep often makes us feel irritable, grumpy and stressed. We will not be able to work to our best and might have difficulty concentrating. Getting enough sleep also boosts our immune system and helps our mental health[ix]. It is generally recommended by health professionals to aim for around seven to nine hours of sleep a night.

It is fairly common to have difficulty sleeping, and there can be various reasons for this. Sometimes it is difficult to sleep if you are worrying about something as your mind might find it difficult to 'switch off' from the worrying thoughts. There can also be physical or environmental reasons for poor sleep. Some basics that help include:

- Make changes to your environment. It can be hard to sleep if it is too hot / cold / noisy / light
- Switch off your phone and electronic devices so that they do not wake you up during the night
- Make a list of things you need to do the next day so that you are not worrying about them
- Go to bed and wake up at the same time each day to help your body get into a good routine
- Relax before you go to bed by reading, listening to relaxing music, doing yoga or another calm activity. This

is more helpful to sleep than watching television or being on the computer later at night. The blue light emitted by screens disrupts sleep-inducing hormones

- Try to avoid drinking caffeine (found in many teas, coffees and fizzy drinks) in the evenings as this acts as a stimulant and makes it more difficult to sleep

---

Activity

If you regularly have difficulty sleeping, speak to a doctor, nurse or counsellor for advice. Try keeping a sleep diary, detailing the times you went to sleep and woke up each night over a week or so. This can be a good starting point for discussion with a health professional. More information on sleep is available from the NHS (www.nhs.uk).

Exercise

Regular exercise is also important. It boosts self-esteem and levels of mental well-being; improves sleep quality and energy levels; and means a lower risk of many illnesses and diseases. Exercise helps us to feel good about ourselves and makes our bodies feel healthier, fitter and stronger.

There are many different types of exercise. Which sound most fun to you?

Walking the dog	Hiking	Running
Swimming	Cycling	Tennis
Badminton	Gymnastics	Dance
Aerobics	Football	Using a gym
Martial Arts	Climbing	Trampolining
Horse Riding	Rowing	Netball
Hockey	Athletics	Volleyball
Exercise Classes	Yoga	Canoeing

| Skiing | Archery | Surfing |
| Ice Skating | Triathlon | Pilates |

Some individuals on the autism spectrum might have found team sports or PE classes at school difficult due to sensory issues, co-ordination difficulties or the emphasis on working with others. Many sports and activities, however, do not have a competitive element. If you can, try out a range of sports at college, university or your local sport centre and decide which suits you best. You do not have to take part in organised sport to get the same health and fitness benefits; walking the dog, walking or cycling instead of driving, or going swimming are just as good.

Activity

If you do not already exercise, identify some sports activities you would like to try out. Find out the times and places you could do these in your local area. What are your next steps? Do you have to book in advance or just turn up? What do you need to wear or take with you? What might get in the way (e.g. lack of confidence, time constraints, feeling too tired) and how could you overcome these?

Trying a new sport

If you decide to go along to a new sports group or exercise class – well done! Introduce yourself to the instructor and tell him / her that it is your first time. They will be happy to help and show you what to do. Do not worry if you cannot keep up for the first few weeks; it often takes a while before you get the hang of things. Try not to be too self-conscious – everybody is more concerned about what they are doing themselves, rather than you. Ask if you are unsure about what to do, and try out a range of classes or groups – all instructors will do things differently and classes will be run for different abilities. It often takes a few attempts before you find a class or group which suits you best.

What to wear

For some sports you will need specialist equipment, but for many all that you need is a pair of trainers and comfortable sports clothing (such as a T-shirt and shorts or joggers). Some sports clothing is made from quick drying material which wicks the sweat away from your skin, keeping you drier and more comfortable. For females, a sports bra can also be a useful purchase – this prevents your breasts from bouncing uncomfortably when you move and can reduce any embarrassment and discomfort this may cause.

Healthy Eating

Eating a healthy and balanced diet is important for both physical and mental well-being. Health professionals generally recommend eating a wide range of foods (including plenty of fruit and vegetables, wholegrain carbohydrates, protein, dairy products and healthy fats) and eating sugary or salty snacks only in moderation. A healthy and balanced diet ensures our body gets all the vitamins, minerals and nutrients it needs to work well and to stay healthy.

Interesting Facts

Although some people skip breakfast, it is generally thought of to be the most important meal of the day. A healthy breakfast gives you energy throughout the morning. People who eat breakfast are also less likely to crave sugary snacks mid-morning.

Making sure you drink enough water is another easy way to improve your health. Many people do not drink enough and dehydration can have negative effects on your health.

Some individuals on the autism spectrum can find it difficult to eat healthily due to sensory preferences and sensitivities. Perhaps there are certain textures, tastes or smells that you cannot bear. This might mean you do not include certain food groups in your diet and miss out on some vital nutrients. If this affects you, speak to your doctor or school nurse and ask for advice.

Further Information

Unfortunately there is a lot of misinformation about exercise, diet and fitness, particularly on the internet. Not everything is true or based on scientific evidence; anybody can write a blog or create a website without being an expert in the field they are writing about. Many of the ideas you will find do not work and could even have a negative effect on your body. It is important to take information only from trustworthy sources. The NHS Live Well website is a good place to start (www.nhs.uk) and ask advice from professionals such as doctors, nurses and other health workers.

Eating Disorders

Eating disorders include anorexia (restricting food intake and not eating enough), bulimia (binge eating and then being deliberately sick) and binge eating disorders (feeling compelled to eat lots of food in a short space of time). A person with an eating disorder may focus unhealthily on their weight and body shape. Eating disorders can be very damaging to a person's physical and mental health.

Eating disorders can occur for many reasons and if you feel you might have an eating disorder it is important to get support as soon as possible. Again, speak to your doctor, a therapist or a family member.

Eating disorders affect a wide range of people and can occur for many different reasons; commonly these can include low self-esteem, a feeling of needing to have control over life, finding it difficult to cope effectively with emotions, and the influence of unrealistic body image. Individuals on the autism spectrum may experience these things, just as anybody else.

There is a lot of misinformation and 'scaremongering' in the media about food; it is important not to take what you read too seriously.

A common autistic trait is the tendency to take things literally or to have 'black and white thinking', and this can also impact eating patterns. Try not to categorise food strictly into 'healthy' and 'unhealthy' categories, or consider food to be either 'good' or 'bad'.   Food cannot be categorised this way; it is often the amount of a certain food, or the way it is cooked which makes it unhealthy. A small amount of chocolate occasionally will not have a negative impact on your health; eating chocolate instead of balanced meals, however, is not so good for you. Another example is potatoes; they are a very nutritious food, but if cooked in lots of oil, become less healthy. Become aware if you find yourself avoiding certain foods; try to consider if you are perhaps being too rigid in your thinking.

Puberty

During puberty your body begins to change and develop from a child's to an adult's body. The average age for a girl to start puberty is around 11 and for boys around 12, but it can happen at any time between the ages of 8 to 14. Puberty can take around four years in total. It can seem quite scary at first, but is perfectly normal and means your body is developing healthily.

What will happen?

For females a number of things will happen during puberty:

- Your breasts will begin to develop
- Pubic hair starts to grow (between your legs)
- Hair begins to grow under your arms and on your legs
- Your periods will start
- You may start to sweat more
- You may begin to get some spots (acne)
- You will go through a growth spurt and reach your adult height
- You will gain weight as your body shape changes from that of a child to a woman

For males, the following things happen:

- Pubic hair starts to appear (at the base of the penis)
- The penis and testicles start to grow and the scrotum gradually becomes darker
- Underarm hair begins to grow
- You begin to sweat more
- You might have 'wet dreams' (involuntary ejaculations of semen as you sleep)
- Your voice will 'break' and become deeper
- You may begin to get some spots (acne)
- You will go through a growth spurt and reach your adult height
- You will begin to become more muscular
- Later, facial hair will begin to grow and you might begin to shave

Remember that not all of these things will happen at once, and most will happen very gradually. You may also experience some mood changes, which again are a very normal response to your body going through all of these changes. Many young people report they feel very self-conscious during this time, have mood swings, or feel low in self-esteem.

Periods

Females begin to get periods during puberty. Your period, or menstrual cycle, is the monthly bleeding from your vagina. Periods usually last 3 – 5 days and happen around once every four weeks, but every female is different. It can take a few years at first for your body to get into a regular cycle.

You can use either sanitary towels or tampons to collect the blood. Both are available from supermarkets, chemists and shops. Sanitary towels have a sticky strip which sticks to the inside of your underwear. Tampons go inside your vagina and collect the blood before it leaves your body. Towels and tampons come in different sizes and you might need to try out different styles and sizes before you find the most comfortable. Remember to change your towel or tampon every few hours, particularly when your period is at its heaviest.

Remember that your period will not start suddenly; at first you may just notice a few drops of blood in your pants. Carry a few towels or tampons in your bag so that you are prepared. If your period starts at school or college, then your school nurse or medical room will have a supply of towels and tampons; do not feel embarrassed about asking for one – that is why they are there!

Some women experience very heavy or painful periods. One of the most common symptoms is stomach cramps. Speak to your doctor or nurse if this affects you as they will be able to recommend suitable medication or other ways of alleviating the pain. Some women also find that exercising can help.

You will be taught about puberty and periods in school and it is also a good idea to talk to somebody - perhaps a parent, relative or older sister, and ask any questions you may have. If you like to read information on the topic independently, there is some information in the next box.

Puberty and autism

Puberty can be a tough time for many young people. Just consider all the things that are happening:

- Your body is going through a lot of physical changes and you have to learn how to cope with these
- You are changing into an adult and developing a lot of new feelings and emotions
- Changes in hormone levels can lead to mood swings
- There are often many other pressures during this time – first you move from primary to secondary school and later you experience more academic pressures such as increased homework and formal exams
- It is a time when you are developing more independence and this can sometimes be tricky to negotiate. You are learning new things and having to make your own decisions. There may also be some conflict with your parents or carers – it can be difficult for them to know how to cope too when their child begins to grow in independence and becomes more grown-up

Remember not to be too hard on yourself. This is a difficult time and life might suddenly feel new and confusing. It is also a very exciting time - you are gaining in independence and have lots of new opportunities ahead.

Some young men and women on the autism spectrum may find puberty a particularly difficult time.[x]

- You might find it particularly upsetting to think of your body changing and not being a child any longer. Change of any sort can be difficult for some people on the autism spectrum
- You might be worried about what to expect and not understand what is going to happen
- You might not feel that you have friends to talk about these things with
- It might be difficult to understand that everybody is going through the same changes and that this is a normal part of growing up

Activity

If you are worried about puberty, make a list of the questions you would like answered. Then speak to a family member, trusted friend or your school nurse, or see if you can find the answers on some of the websites given earlier in this section.

Body image

Body image concerns how you view your physical self – how you think and feel about your body, your appearance or your looks. Somebody with a negative body image may have thoughts such as:

'I'm so ugly.'

'I'm too fat / thin / tall / short / spotty.'

'I hate my body.'

'I wear baggy clothes to hide my body.'

'I spend hours looking in the mirror and worrying how I look.'

Whereas somebody with a more positive body image would have thoughts such as:

'I'm not perfect, but nobody is. I'm just me.'

'I'm happy with myself and that's what counts. It doesn't matter what other people think.'

'I'm never going to be tall, blonde and thin but that doesn't matter. It's ultimately who I am as a person that is important.'

'I appreciate my body for keeping me strong, healthy and energetic, not just the way it looks.'

Body image can be closely linked to self-esteem. Having a negative body image can be common in teenagers and young people. There are several reasons for this:

- You are going through puberty and your body is changing. This can be difficult to get used to. You might find you compare yourself to others. It is important to remember not everybody grows at the same time in the same way.
- There are lots of images all around us (on television, in magazines, on the internet) of celebrities which suggest that there is a 'right' way to look – these women are often tall, thin, have long thick hair, tanned skin and heavy make-up. Men are often tall, muscular and clear-skinned. It can be easy to compare ourselves negatively to these images. In real life, these people do not actually look this good. Most images we are presented with have been airbrushed or photoshopped to make those individuals appear thinner, spot-free or wrinkle-free. Make sure you are not comparing yourself with unrealistic images.

- You might pick up from family or friends that there is a 'right' way to look. Different groups and cultures can have certain fashions or trends which they wish to emulate.
- Many magazines / internet sites also have headlines about losing weight or getting a 'perfect body'. It is important to remember that these 'quick fixes' and 'miracle diets' do not work – if they did, the media would not have to keep promoting new ones! Magazines, websites and other advertisers play on people's low self-esteem and worries to entice them to buy their products.
- Many people believe that changing their appearance will make them happier or will help them to fit in. The fashion and beauty industries often try to suggest that having an 'ideal' body image will make you more successful and happier in all aspects of your life. It is far better to work on your self-esteem, assertiveness, and confidence. If you feel good on the inside, you will appear confident and attractive on the outside.

When we are surrounded by all of these images and ideas, it can be difficult to maintain a good sense of body image. Having a negative body image can have a negative impact. You might spend hours worrying or obsessing about your body, it may stop you from doing things or going out, and it can contribute to low self-esteem and a lack of confidence.

What can you do if you are worried about your body image?

- Firstly, remember that eating a balanced diet, keeping active, and getting enough sleep will help you to stay healthy and to feel good about yourself.
- Wear clothing that you feel comfortable in – this will help you to feel more confident. Remember to stand up tall and straight – this improves confidence!
- If you are female, as your breasts begin to grow you will need to start wearing a bra. Wearing the right size will

ensure your breasts are supported and stay in the right place. Many department stores offer a bra-fitting service to help you to find the right size.

- Remember that the vast majority of images that you see in the media have been altered; they are not true reflections of how other people look.
- Speak to somebody about your worries and concerns – this may be a family member, school counsellor or school nurse.

Mental and Emotional Wellbeing

We have discussed various aspects of physical health; now it is time to turn to mental and emotional wellbeing.

Activity

At the end of each day note in your journal two or three things that you are grateful for. These can be big or small. This has been shown to be a good way of improving mood[xi] and reminding ourselves of all of the good things in our lives.

Examples:

'Having the opportunity to go to dance club and having fun there'

'Spending time playing with my new kitten'

'Being able to get an education'

'Having a kind classmate who lent me a pen'

Mental and emotional wellbeing involves our thoughts, feelings and emotions. Sometimes these can be overwhelming and can lead to us feeling depressed, anxious, stressed or worried. This can prevent us from carrying out our daily activities, learning well, or from enjoying life.

Many people experience difficulties with their mental or emotional health at some point in their lives. For individuals on the autism spectrum there might be some specific reasons for this[xii]:

- You might feel different from other people, interpret the world differently and might not understand why
- Other people might not understand your autism so you can feel misunderstood. Other people's negative reactions can also contribute to feelings of low self-esteem and not being good enough
- You might have difficulties communicating with others. You might internalise difficulties rather than discuss them, which can cause greater problems
- Having a tendency to take things literally can cause misunderstandings
- Liking to spend time alone or finding it difficult to make friends, might lead to experiencing feelings of loneliness and might mean you do not have others to share your feelings with
- Difficulty in understanding the perspective of other people can cause misunderstandings. Some individuals on the autism spectrum also find that they respond differently to feelings than other people, for example, they might laugh at something upsetting or cry when they are angry. This can make it more difficult to learn how to identify and manage emotions
- You might have difficulty in understanding your own feelings and emotions

- Other people may have difficulty in identifying how you are feeling as you might be less expressive than some non-autistics. Some individuals on the autism spectrum might find that their emotions are mis-labelled by others and that these labels do not match their inner experience (e.g. somebody might say, '*You must be feeling so disappointed!*' but really you are feeling relief or something completely different)
- Some unkind people might not be tolerant of differences. You might experience direct or indirect bullying, prejudice or discrimination
- Often services and policies have not been designed with autistic people in mind

However, the positive thing is that there is also a lot you can do to improve your sense of mental wellbeing. Sometimes, in fact, it can help just to become more aware of some of the differences and difficulties listed above; this can help your understanding of situations.

Activity

Continue to write or draw in your journal regularly to help you to reflect on your feelings, emotions and reactions in different situations. Sometimes it may help to follow a structure (you will not always need to answer all of the questions):

What happened?

How did I feel? What was I thinking? How did I act?

How do I feel now, after the situation?

What are my options now? Which would be best?

What have I learned from this situation?

Could I try anything differently next time?

Feelings and emotions

We all experience many different feelings every single day! This is completely normal. Here are just a few words that can describe feelings:

Happy	Sad	Disgusted	Shocked
Surprised	Angry	Relieved	Upset
Excited	Grateful	Disappointed	Satisfied
Irritated	Frustrated	Pleased	Proud
Anxious	Worried	Frightened	Calm
Hope	Awe	Inspiration	Amusement

Which other words can you add to the list?

Activity

If you enjoy reading fiction, this can be a great way of increasing your feelings vocabulary. You will come across many words that describe feelings and emotions, as well as understanding more about how others feel in different situations. If you enjoy watching film or television, you will also see actors portraying a range of emotions. Can you tell which feeling they are portraying from their body language and facial expression?

Some individuals on the autism spectrum can find it difficult to recognise and respond to emotions in themselves and in others. The medical term for this is alexithymia. You might, for example, find it difficult to recognise how others are feeling, might not pick up on body language or facial expression, or might have been told that you are not particularly expressive. You might find it difficult to label your feelings or to know how to respond (There is more about communication and empathy in Section 3 of this book).

It can help simply to become aware of some of your differences and difficulties. If you begin to realise why some of these misunderstandings occur then it can help you to understand and accept them.

Let's look at an example:

When upset some individuals on the autism spectrum need to be left alone to cope with their feelings and to begin to feel better. In this state it might impossible to interact or communicate with other people. In fact, just having other people around might make you feel a whole lot worse. This might cause some problems because many non-autistics like to comfort people who are upset; they like to hug them, talk to them and, for some of them, having people around can be a great source of comfort. You can see how misunderstanding might occur; people are intending to be helpful but are in fact making the situation worse.

However, just being aware of this can make all the difference. You can tell people you realise they just want to help and thank them for their concern, but can state you need to have some time alone.

Your own preferences may be different from the example above – there is only space in this book to cover one or two possibilities. Over time you will learn more about your own preferences and needs and this will enable you to manage them more effectively.

Activity

Many people say or think 'I'll be happy when...(I pass my exam / I have a boyfriend / I earn more money)'. Do you ever find yourself thinking like this?

This style of thinking can be unhelpful as you then begin to rely on external events, such as getting a boyfriend or more money, for your happiness. In reality, these things only bring short-lived happiness. We are still the same person with the same way of interpreting the world. Instead of saying 'I'll be happy when...' choose to say 'I'm happy now because...'. Find the positives in your current situation.

Emotional Intelligence

Emotional intelligence is the term used to describe the ability to recognise, understand and manage feelings and emotions. Everybody, whether on the autism spectrum or not, continues to improve their emotional intelligence throughout adolescence and adulthood.

The good news is that everybody can increase their emotional intelligence. If you go to your local library or bookstore you will find row upon row of self-help book. There are books on emotional intelligence, on how to become happier, on how to reduce anger or stress, on how to alleviate depression and anxiety, and on how to be more confident, successful or joyful – you are not the only person wanting to learn more about these things!

If you feel emotional intelligence is an area you would benefit from working on, there are various steps you can take:

- Reflect on your thoughts, feelings and emotions in your journal
- Reflect on and learn from experience
- Discuss your thoughts and feelings with trusted friends or relatives
- Try out strategies from self-help books (some available are aimed specifically at individuals on the autism spectrum)
- Speak to a counsellor / therapist / coach and use strategies she or he suggests
- Take part in a course which supports you to develop these skills (you might find your college, university, or local autism service offer these)

Emotions cannot simply be categorised into 'positive' and 'negative' Humans experience a range of emotions for good reasons. Feeling afraid, for example, helps us to remove ourselves from danger. It is normal to feel anxious, disappointed, sad and a whole range of emotions depending on the situation we are in. Learn to accept your feelings and emotions without judging them. Think to yourself, 'I'm feeling .... That's ok.'

Activity

Sometimes, emotions can feel overwhelming. Perhaps you feel full of anger, frustration or confusion. At these times there are things you can do to help yourself feel calmer. Do any of the activities listed below work for you? Perhaps you could try some.

Bouncing on a trampoline? Going for a walk? Playing sport? Dancing? Spending time with a pet? Swimming? Running? Drawing? Colouring in? Painting? Listening to music? Gardening? Talking to a friend? Having a bath? Sleep? Slow breathing? Hitting a punch bag? Writing it down? Reading? Playing an instrument?

Your aim should not be to eliminate more 'negative' feelings completely, but to learn how to cope with them more effectively. We will always experience a range of emotions and this is part of being human. A more realistic aim is to learn how to cope more effectively with a range of emotions.

Worry

We all worry about things at times. Sometimes this is helpful. If we are worried about doing well in an exam, for example, this worry might motivate us to revise for it.

Sometimes, however, too much worry can be unhelpful. We might spend a lot of time worrying about something that has already happened in the past, or something that has not yet happened. We might worry about making a decision if we are unsure which option to choose.

Activity

Different strategies work for different people when it comes to coping with worry. You might find that writing your worries down helps you to make sense of your thoughts and then allows you to concentrate on doing other things.

Some people set aside 'worry time'. When they catch themselves worrying they think, 'I will worry about that between 6 and 6.30 this evening'. Often, when that time comes around, the worry has already diminished.

Having to make a decision can also be fatiguing, particularly as some people on the autism spectrum have difficulty in predicting their feelings. Try writing down the pros and cons of each option. Sometimes people feel better for having made a decision, even if they are not 100% sure they have made the right choice. Most decisions can be reversed if you realised you made the wrong choice at a later date.

Stimming

Stimming is the name given to making repetitive movements or repetitive sounds. Individuals on the autism spectrum might 'stim' to feel calmer and reduce anxiety. For some it can help with focus and to counteract overwhelming sensory environments. Stimming behaviours can include hand flapping, rocking or repetitively feeling certain textures. Plenty of non-autistics 'stim' in a way too – but often these behaviours may be a little less obvious, such as nail-biting, hair twirling and foot tapping.

Identify if you 'stim' and what methods you use. Generally it isn't a problem but some loud or large stimming behaviours may be less acceptable when you are in certain environments (e.g. when you are in a lecture or work meeting and other people are trying to concentrate).

Optimism, resilience and a growth mindset

Being optimistic means having a positive mental attitude about the future; you are hopeful and confident that things will be successful or work out. Being pessimistic is roughly the opposite; you assume that everything is going to turn out negatively.

Sometimes, a bit of pessimism is helpful if we act on it. If, for example, you identify things that could go wrong in a situation, you can think about how to solve these problems in advance and will be better prepared for different eventualities. However, too much pessimism can mean you focus on all of the negatives; this might lead to a lack of motivation and loss of enthusiasm.

If you feel you have a tendency to be pessimistic, train yourself to be a little more optimistic. Try to find positives in different situations and events, rather than just focussing on the negatives. Consider what went well and what you have learned. There is a well-known saying, 'Every cloud has a silver lining'. This just means that in every negative or difficult situation, there is likely to be a positive too – you just have to find it!

Think about the two examples that follow:

1. You were looking forward to going to the cinema with your friend but she is ill so you have to postpone. The positive might be that you are able to spend the evening completing an assignment that you needed to get finished. You experience a sense of accomplishment and when your friend is feeling better you enjoy your trip to the cinema as you do not have to worry about the assignment you need to complete.
2. You do not do as well as you would have liked in a university essay. You might be disappointed but this might encourage you to focus on how to improve your next essay and on learning how to develop more effective study techniques.

Resilience

Resilience means having the ability to 'bounce back' from difficult or negative situations. It means coping successfully with everyday problems in life, rather than letting them overwhelm us[xiii]. Somebody who is not very resilient might give up easily when faced with a problem or difficulty. Resilience is an important life skill and can help us in our personal and social lives as well as in education and employment.

Activity

Many of the activities in this book will help you to develop your resilience. Note in your journal when you feel you overcome problems successfully. What did you do that was successful?

You could also try to use some step-by-step planning techniques to help you to achieve your goals – some examples of these are included in section 6 of this book.

Mindfulness

You might have encountered the concept of 'mindfulness'. Mindfulness is based on ancient Buddhist techniques and basically means being more aware of the present moment and your current situation. It means observing carefully and non-judgementally what is going on in your body and mind and noticing events (internal and external) in an open, inquisitive manner. This enables you to be less 'tangled up' in your thoughts and emotions.

If you are interested, you might find mindfulness sessions are available in your college, workplace or local community, and you should look for those taught by qualified practitioners. Here are some simple exercises that can also help you to become more mindful in the meantime:

- Take time to focus on your environment. Observe the things around you closely – flowers, trees, insects,

55

animals, patterns, objects. Focus on the object and try to find details that you have never noticed before. Try not to make a judgement, simply observe

- Take a few moments to close your eyes and to listen carefully. Which sounds can you identify that you were not aware of?
- Take some long, slow breaths in and out. Focus solely on your breath and how it fills your body. If your thoughts wander, do not worry. Simply bring your attention back to your breathing
- If you are walking or taking public transport, try to observe three things you have never noticed before. Or maybe choose a colour and try to notice everything in your environment of that colour
- Be curious about your thoughts and opinions, and those of others. Try not to judge. Think instead, *'I'm having the thought that…'*

Activity

It is often small, unexpected things that make us happier than big gestures. Which little things bring you joy? Spending time with your pet? Laughing at funny jokes? Clean bed sheets? A bunch of fresh flowers on the table? Make an effort to notice these things.

This section has suggested some activities to help your general sense of mental wellbeing and ability to cope with everyday life. However, for some people, mental health problems can become more serious, having a long-term negative effect on their lives. Again, this is not uncommon – some estimates suggest that more than 1 in 4 people will experience a mental health difficulty at some point in their lives.

Autism spectrum conditions are not mental health difficulties in themselves. Many individuals on the autism spectrum have a good sense of wellbeing and would consider themselves to be very happy people.[xiv]

Remember that autism cannot be 'treated' by medication. However, some individuals on the autism spectrum may experience other difficulties (such as anxiety, depression, or attention deficit hyperactivity disorder) which might be treated by medication.

Some mental health conditions are treated by medication which can help to ease symptoms. Others may be treated by talking therapies, and some by a combination of the two.

If you are prescribed medication for a mental health condition, there can be many questions and concerns you might have about this. A useful website is HeadMeds (www.headmeds.org.uk) which is aimed specifically at younger people who want to find out more about the medication they are taking.

Further Information

Speak to somebody if you are concerned about worrying thoughts or feelings. Look at the list included at the end of section one in this book to help you to identify who would be most appropriate to approach.

Useful websites about mental wellbeing and mental health include Young Minds, Mind and the NHS.

Other sources of support include ChildLine (www.childline.org.uk) for under 19s, and the Samaritans (www.samaritans.org). You can speak about your concerns confidentially over the phone or via email.

Something you didn't
expect to enjoy, but did…

Something that brightens
your day…

Scribble Page…

Something that makes
you laugh…

Something you are
looking forward to…

Friendships, relationships and communication

Section 3: Friendships, relationships and communication

Friendships, relationships and communication can often cause difficulties for individuals on the autism spectrum. This is a key feature of autism – differences in connecting to other people on a social and emotional level.

Interesting Fact

The word autism itself comes from the Greek word 'autos' which means 'self'.

In this section we look at a number of issues, including communication, conversational skills, assertiveness, friendships, empathy, relationships and sexuality.

Communication

Let's start with communication - how we give, share and receive information. Communication can be one-way (e.g. a poster, a written letter or a speech) or two-way (e.g. face-to-face conversation, skype or a telephone conversation). Communication can be spoken or written.

Spoken Communication

We use many skills when we talk to others. We:

- Use eye contact
- Use gesture (e.g. hand movement)
- Use body language to show we are listening (e.g. facing towards the speaker and not moving around too much)
- Keep an appropriate distance from other people – not standing too close or too far away
- Speak at an appropriate volume – not too loud and not too quietly
- Speak at an appropriate pace – not too slowly and not too quickly
- Speak clearly

- Vary our tone of voice to make our speech more interesting and less 'robotic'
- Use words that the listeners understand
- Start and finish a conversation
- Take turns to speak
- Interrupt politely
- Listen and respond carefully to what other people say
- Use facial expression to show that we are listening and have understood
- Use facial expression to add to the meaning of what we are saying
- Ask other people appropriate questions
- Answer questions appropriately
- Seek clarification and ask when unsure
- Express our thoughts and opinions
- Understand what other people say
- Stay on topic
- Change topic appropriately
- Take it in turns to speak and ensure everybody can contribute
- Move the conversation forward
- Help other people join in the conversation
- Take other people's feelings and perspectives into consideration
- Avoid offending others
- Use an appropriate level of formality and politeness

That is a lot to think about! Individuals on the autism might have differences in some of the areas listed above.[xv]

I didn't know that eye contact was important until somebody explained it to me!

I find it difficult to keep up in group conversations and to know what to say.

> I've been told that I am not very expressive in my face and tone of voice.

> Other people always seem to misinterpret what I say. I can't seem to express what I intend to.

Activity

How would you rate your spoken communication skills? Look at the list above. Rate yourself from 1 – 5 for each one (1= not very good at this, 5 = very good at this). You could record this in your notebook or journal. Maybe you could ask your family, trusted friends or a teacher what they think too. Do you have initial thoughts on any areas you would like to improve?

There are many ways of improving your conversational skills if this is an area you would like to develop. You might start by watching and observing others, in real-life and on screen. See if you can identify what successful communicators do. If you enjoy learning independently, many books are available on communication skills; look in your local library or bookstore.

Your school, college, university or speech and language therapist might offer a social communication group where you can work with a small group of other students to develop your skills. Some individuals on the autism spectrum find taking part in drama classes or foreign language lessons are also beneficial. These can be safe spaces to role play and to learn about the mechanics of communication techniques in more detail. They can also be a lot of fun!

Quick Tip

If you find eye contact uncomfortable, try looking at the other person for just a second or two, and then look away. Alternatively, try focusing on a point between their eyebrows.

Often, context makes spoken communication difficult[xvi] . It can be easy to learn the various skills listed above in isolation, but far more difficult to apply these in practice. It takes time and perseverance, but is a skill worth mastering.

The importance of communication

Communication is important, even if you are a solitary person and enjoy your own company. Being able to communicate effectively makes daily life easier. Communicating clearly and assertively means fewer misunderstandings and less anxiety.

General tips for conversation

Conversation is complex! There is a lot to think about and it can take time to develop good conversational skills. A few general strategies include:

- Smile when you meet other people. Introduce yourself if you have not met before (*'Hi. My name's Kate. What's yours?'*). Evidence suggests people make an initial judgement of another person within the first few seconds of meeting them[xvii]. Making a positive first impression might mean we receive a more positive response from others
- Ask somebody's name if you do not know it (*'I don't think we've met before. I'm Kate. What's your name?'*)
- Ask for further information or ask when you do not understand what somebody has said (*'Sorry, could you repeat that? I didn't quite hear you.' 'I don't know much about abseiling. What does that involve?'*)
- Show that you are listening to other people by looking in their direction
- Many conversations begin with a greeting and asking, *'How are you?'* This is often not the time to go into great detail. You might answer with *'Good, thank you. And you?'*
- Sometimes conversations begin with 'small talk'. This is general chit-chat which often does not mean a lot, but is

important. It allows people to 'warm up' into the conversation and get to know each other. You might comment, for example, on non-controversial topics such as the weather, the traffic, or your journey

- Different topics are suitable for different conversations. At work with customers and clients, or with people you do not know well, you would not discuss personal topics such as your health problems or family troubles. These topics are more suitable to discuss with closer friends or family members
- You do not have to give information you do not feel comfortable sharing. If somebody asks a question you are uncomfortable with, you could say something like, *'I don't know, I've never really thought about that before'*, *'I don't really feel comfortable talking about that at the moment'*, or *'I think I'd have to have more information before I form an opinion on that'*
- Misunderstandings happen all of the time in conversation! In fact, many television sitcoms and comedy shows are based on this sort of mix-up. Have you ever watched a sketch where two characters are talking at cross purposes? It can be very funny to watch but very confusing when it happens in real life! Be open and honest if this happens and show willing to 'repair' the conversation (*'I think we may be talking about two different things here'*, *'I'm sorry, I think I may have misunderstood what you said. Can you explain it again?'*, or *'Sorry, I misheard you! I thought you said …!'*)

Conversation skills

Do you find anything difficult about taking part in conversations? Perhaps you find it difficult to keep up with what is going on? Maybe it is difficult to know when to speak? Perhaps you have been accused of being rude or unfriendly when this was not your intention? Perhaps you find it difficult to know what to contribute; it can seem as if everybody else has had the script beforehand and knows exactly what to say! It can seem astonishing at times how other people manage to make conversation and just talk about nothing!

Some individuals on the autism spectrum might only feel the need to communicate with others when there is a clear purpose. In comparison, many non-autistics (or 'neurotypicals') communicate and talk to each other often without a clear purpose in mind; just as a way to pass the time or to cement their relationship. Some people on the autism spectrum might feel anxious around others so do not find this sort of 'chatting' as relaxing or as enjoyable as others do.

Some autistic individuals find it easier to communicate if there is a clear purpose (e.g. having to ask when the next train leaves, or dealing with a customer at work), may still find it more difficult to take part in general conversation.

Sometimes, 'neuro-typical' conversation can be especially confusing. Many people (but certainly not all) often enjoy conversations in which they share feelings and emotions; and in which they discuss a topic from many different perspectives, rather than reach a firm conclusion. This can be particularly confusing to some individuals on the autism spectrum who prefer to have a clear outcome and 'point' to the conversation. There is nothing wrong with either method; they are just two different ways of communicating.[xviii]

Male and female conversation

Some evidence suggests that some females on the autism spectrum are perhaps more expressive (in gesture, facial expression and tone of voice) than males on the autism spectrum[xix]. In addition, some females on the autism spectrum have very good conversational and social skills; again something not traditionally associated with autism! Some research indicates that many females on the autism spectrum are more able to copy and mimic others and to pick up on social rules and expectations than their male counterparts[xx]. You might feel you have good communication skills on one level but still do not connect with others in the same way.

Activity

Everybody has different communication strengths and weaknesses. Some of the examples above may not reflect your personal experiences. Start to note in your journal any communication experiences which you find easy or enjoy, and any situations you find more difficult.

The ease of communication often depends on who we are interacting with. Sometimes it may be that you are communicating with other people who have less developed communication skills themselves. Do not always blame yourself if there are situations you find particularly difficult or confusing.

Taking things literally

A difference often associated with those on the autism spectrum is a greater tendency to take things literally; this can sometimes make communication more difficult.

Humour and sarcasm might be difficult to recognise at times; these things are usually identified by the context, or by a change in tone of voice or expression. Idioms and other figurative language can also be difficult to understand; these elements of language do not have a literal meaning. Have you ever heard or read phrases such as:

'It's raining cats and dogs!'

'Driving a car? That's a piece of cake!'

'Cycling just isn't my cup of tea.'

Language is full of idioms, metaphors and similes such as these. Many have interesting origins. Sometimes you will be able to work out the meaning of idioms and metaphors from the context. Others you may need to ask about or look up on the internet or in a dictionary. There are also books available which explain the meaning of common idioms and metaphors.

Some individuals on the autism spectrum can have a literal understanding and assume that other people mean exactly what they say when. In fact, people often (confusingly) do not mean what they say. Look at these examples:

When somebody says, 'I'll phone you back in five minutes', they might not mean exactly five minutes. It might be in ten minutes, or as soon as they have finished doing another task. In these cases, people often give an approximation of a time-frame or distance.

When somebody says, 'We'll have to meet up for a drink sometime', they might not necessarily mean this. They might do, but they may also just be speaking out of habit, out of politeness, or trying to find a way to end the conversation quickly. It all depends on context.

Other people might mean what they say, but simply forget that they have said something. This happens frequently; people are busy and have many things to keep in their minds. Somebody might say, 'I'll lend you that book', but then simply forgets all about it.

Others might simply not even realise what they are saying! In conversation, some people agree with others, simply because they do not wish to disagree openly, appear different or because their mind is elsewhere. Some people can be uncomfortable with silences in conversation so say something quickly to 'fill the gap'. This might be the first thing that comes into their head and not necessarily the truth.

In fact, people say things they do not mean all of the time! To some individuals on the autism spectrum who take things literally and often have good memories for detail, this can seem as if people are not being honest. It can make other people seem unpredictable, confusing and untrustworthy! It can also cause considerable anxiety and can lead to worry about something unnecessarily or believing something which does not turn out to be true. Have you ever found yourself saying or thinking things like, 'But you said...!', or 'But that's not what she said the other day!'

It can also be difficult for some individuals on the autism spectrum to understand 'gossip'. Take an example: You might hear two colleagues talk negatively about another, yet when the third one enters the room, the other two are very pleasant to her face. Do these two like her or dislike her? Will these two begin talking negatively about you when you leave the room? How can you possibly know what people really think?

Situations like this tend to be difficult for those on the autism spectrum. It is difficult to understand other people's beliefs and intentions, and to accept that everybody has different perceptions of the same situation.

Sometimes individuals on the autism spectrum are accused of being 'too honest', of perhaps pointing out others' mistakes, or of saying things that are inappropriate to the situation. The cause is often having taken things literally or having remembered things that others have long forgotten!

Activity

Reflect on breakdowns in communication that you experience. Can you identify why the misunderstanding might have occurred?

Teach yourself not to worry about things that people say. Not everybody means what they say. Over time you will become better at understanding other people.

Note your communication strengths too. Some individuals on the autism spectrum find it much easier to communicate on a one-to-one basis, rather than in a larger group. Others are good at

---

presenting in front of an audience, or can communicate well through writing. Work to your strengths when you can.

Assertiveness

You might have heard people talk about being assertive, but what exactly does it mean?

When we respond to a situation, we can usually respond in one of three ways: aggressively, assertively or passively.

An aggressive response can involve anger, violence and physical or verbal attacks. It might include sarcasm or attempt to hurt the other person in some way. An aggressive response does not respect other people and may include shouting, swearing, threatening or acting as if you are better than others.

A passive response often involves saying or doing nothing. It lacks confidence and avoids the problem. A passive response involves keeping your feelings to yourself and allowing others to treat you with disrespect. You may speak quietly, say nothing, make yourself look small, go along with things you are uncomfortable with, or act as if you are not as important as other people.

An assertive response is in the middle of these two extremes. It involves expressing your thoughts and feelings honestly and openly. It respects both yourself and the other person and allows you to exercise your personal rights without denying the rights of others.

Individuals who are assertive are generally more able to resolve conflict, take control of their own lives, be more confident in their ability to achieve, make more positive choices, and are more able to say 'no' to peer pressure. They are also less likely to be victims of aggression or bullying. Being assertive is a sought-after skill which many people find difficult; there are many courses and books available which look at this in more detail.

Tips on being assertive

- Keep calm and use a low, clear and steady voice
- Stand up tall and still
- Look at the other person to show you are listening to their point of view
- Use 'I' statements to describe how you feel (*'I feel … when you … because …. I would like…'*)
- Respect your own feelings and those of other people
- Do not feel that you have to keep justifying your reasons, just remain polite and firm

Being assertive takes practice but it is a useful skill to master as it can help to reduce anxiety and worry. Here is an example:

Perhaps your friends enjoy going out to nightclubs, partying all night and staying out late; this is just not your thing. You do not enjoy these situations and feel uncomfortable, however, you do not like to say 'no' to them, so worry about it for the whole week, do not enjoy the evening and afterwards wish you had not gone out. When you try to say that you do not want to go, you feel as if they continue to pressure you in to it.

A more assertive response to this situation might be: *'Thank you for inviting me, but nightclubbing just isn't really my thing. Please don't try to keep persuading me to join in because I know I will go away and worry about it. I do hope you enjoy the evening though.'* This way you remain polite, respect their feelings and your own. A good follow-up could be to make a suggestion that perhaps the following week you could go to the cinema one evening or do an activity which you enjoy more, so that you are still able to spend some time with your friends, but are not stopping them from doing activities they enjoy.

Socialising with others

Activity

Think about how you get on with others. How do you feel when you are around people? Are you more comfortable in some situations than others? Do you find some people easier to get on with than others? Why do you think this is?

Autism is not simply 'being an introvert'. Everybody is somewhere along the introvert – extrovert scale, with introverts preferring their own company and finding the company of others exhausting, and extroverts feeling energised by mixing with others.[xxi] Autism is a deeper difference in connecting with others and interpreting the social world. Sometimes it is described as not having an innate desire to connect with others, or feeling like an alien living on a planet of another species!

Perhaps you feel uncomfortable or anxious around other people? Perhaps you do not see the point of socialising; it might seem very 'fake'? Or maybe you just feel exhausted after being with other people? These can all be common amongst individuals on the autism spectrum.

Other differences sometimes identified by individuals on the autism spectrum can include:

- Needing more time alone and time to 'recover' after socialising
- Finding it difficult to discuss emotions; perhaps even feeling like an 'emotional robot' when with others
- Not 'getting' group emotions, responding to events in a different way emotionally

- Having delayed emotional processing, needing time to identify emotions; an event may have passed for others but you may still be processing it
- Feeling 'invisible' in groups
- Difficulty in understanding how other people may perceive you
- Difficulty in understanding the perspective of others
- Being 'too honest' and not being influenced by social pretences and conventions; perhaps being perceived as being tactless
- 'Fitting in' not being as important to you as to others; not being influenced so much by current trends, fashions and social norms

Improving your communication skills and assertiveness can help you to gain confidence to cope in social situations. This can help to reduce anxiety and ensures you feel more relaxed.

Activity

What do you appreciate and admire about other people? Think about the people who you know and write in your journal about the qualities they have that you admire.

Example:

My friend Jacinta for her enthusiasm and inclusive attitude.

Friendships

Friendships are important for many people. Friends are those who we share experiences with, talk to about our hopes and concerns, have fun with and ask for advice. Friends offer support and they are people we can trust. Having supportive friends around can make life easier and more enjoyable.

All friendships are different and are often based on some shared interests, experiences or values. Sometimes we have friends for just a short time before growing apart or moving away; other friendships may last throughout our lives. Sometimes we have friends in one particular situation (e.g. at work or at rowing club) but we might not see these friends outside of this situation.

Different groups of friends also have different 'norms'. Some female friends are very demonstrative, often hugging and air-kissing for example, while others are not. Some friends are constantly in touch with each other, while others just have a good catch up when they see each other. It really does not matter what 'style' of friendship you have; just find what works for you.

Interesting Facts

Sometimes individuals on the autism spectrum find it easier to make friends with people older or younger than themselves. It is only in the school system where there is an emphasis on making friends who are exactly the same age.

Friendships might be particularly difficult at school or college because there is a limited group of people who you are expected to make friends with. This is also a time when everybody is learning how to make friends and form relationships; teenagers are only just establishing their own identity and there can be lots of pressure to go along with the crowd.

It can become easier to make friends as you become older. People generally become more tolerant and less concerned about peer pressure and 'fitting in'.

Some individuals on the autism spectrum find it difficult to have more than one friend at a time. Others can find that their friendships become quite intense. Some of their friends might tell them they would like a less intense friendship.

Being on the autism spectrum you might wonder if you will find it easier to make friends with other autistic individuals than with neuro-typicals (non-autistics). You might have some characteristics in common with others on the autism spectrum and may find you share similar experiences, but this does not necessarily guarantee that you will become good friends (just as there is no guarantee that any two neurotypicals will become the best of friends). Ultimately, good friends accept you for who you are and enjoy your company, regardless of whether you (or they) are autistic or not.

Activity

Who are your friends? What have been your experiences of friendships so far?

In relation to your autism, can you identify any differences in how you connect with other people? Does finding out you are on the autism spectrum help to explain any friendship difficulties you may have experienced in the past?

Sometimes it can be difficult to get to know people enough to become friends. You might have to make an effort to go to groups, clubs and social events to get to know people. Friendships often develop over time; we get to know somebody and become comfortable in their presence. You might be able to articulate clearly how you connect with others and what your differences are, or it might be an area that you have not considered before. Your experiences connecting to other people are likely to be very individual, and many factors can play a role. You may have been fortunate to have met people who are kind, tolerant and accepting. You might also have met people who have not been understanding. Your past experiences are likely to contribute to how you view others.

Activity

Make a list of what you think people want in a friend.

You might have included some of the following:

Reliability – somebody who does what they promise to

Trustworthy – the ability to keep a secret and keep promises

Honest – telling the truth

Interested – taking an interest in their friend's hobbies, interests, work or family

Supportive – helping when you need support

A good listener – somebody who remembers what you tell them.

There are many other things that could also be added. Remember that friendship is a two-way process. If you want somebody to be a good friend to you, you will need to be a good friend to them in return.

Friendships can be difficult at times – plenty of people fall out with friends, are hurt by friends, or just grow apart over time. People are complex and constantly changing; misunderstandings are inevitable from time to time.

Toxic Friendships

There might be times when you find yourself surrounded by people who do not make you feel good. Perhaps you do not really like these people, feel uncomfortable around them or feel they are unkind or manipulating you. Perhaps they put pressure on you, or use manipulative behaviours such as threats, sarcasm, sulking, the silent treatment, or trying to make you feel guilty. Unfortunately there are some deliberately unkind people around, and some who are just unaware of the impact of their behaviour on others.

Empathy / Theory of Mind

A topic find often discussed with autism is that of empathy, or theory of mind. Those on the autism spectrum are often considered to have differences in these areas.

'Theory of Mind' is the psychological term used to describe the ability to be able to see things from the perspective of other people. It is the ability to recognise that other people have thoughts, beliefs, abilities, feelings and perspectives different to our own.

'Empathy' is the experience of understanding another person's position from their perspective. You 'put yourself in their shoes' and feel what they are feeling.[xxiii]

Just because empathy or theory of mind skills might not come naturally to you, it does not mean that you lack these skills completely, or that you are not a kind, caring and thoughtful person. Consider the following:

- Often it is simply a question of perspective. Neurotypicals find it just as difficult to understand individuals on the autism spectrum as the other way around! So, it is not only those on the autism spectrum who have theory of mind difficulties. As children we are often taught to 'treat others how you wish to be treated', yet this does not take into account that everybody has different preferences and needs. People often find it easier to empathise with others who are similar to themselves, rather than those who are different.
- Sometimes individuals on the autism spectrum have difficulties with expressing empathy, rather than feeling it. Sometimes difficulties are with using the appropriate facial expressions, body language and words.
- Individuals on the autism spectrum connect differently on a social level, so some difficulties can come about because they might not be as concerned with the

'unwritten social agreement' in place as others. Some things valued by others might seem superficial or meaningless. It can be difficult to comprehend why others are worrying about certain issues.

- Everybody lies somewhere along the empathy scale; there are many people to whom this just does not come naturally. Empathy levels are not fixed; many people become more empathetic over time, perhaps after different life experiences.

Interesting Facts

Reading fiction has been shown to be a good way of enhancing theory of mind as it gives readers a better insight into the thoughts, feelings and actions of others.[xxiv]

Some recent evidence suggests that young people in general are becoming less empathetic. Modern lifestyles, more screen time and fewer face-to-face interactions have been blamed.

It can often be difficult to understand other people's feelings, perspectives and actions. This is because we are all different, have all had different upbringings and life experiences. We all have different beliefs, religions, values, hopes and dreams. Often we cannot understand another person completely; we have to accept that they are who they are and we are who we are.

Relationships

From friendships we turn to the matter of closer relationships. For many people a close, intimate relationship with another person is important at some point in their lives. For some individuals on the autism spectrum, however, having a close relationship is not important. If so, that is fine – simply enjoy being single!

Close relationships can be great, but can also be a huge source of conflict and anguish at times. Just look at all the books, films, television shows, magazines and blogs based on relationship problems!

Some specific areas which may cause difficulty for some individuals on the autism spectrum:

- To get to know somebody well you have to be committed to spending time with them and learning about them; this can be difficult if you prefer to spend considerable time alone, like to engage in special interests or to follow a rigid routine
- If you do not enjoy socialising in 'traditional' ways it might be more difficult to meet others
- Differences in communication can sometimes create difficulties
- You might be uncomfortable with, or extra sensitive to, sensory issues such as intimate touch and being in close physical proximity to others
- You might have questions about your gender or sexuality
- Differences in theory of mind abilities can lead to misunderstandings, confusion or unequal relationships

Activity

In your journal, reflect on your experiences, if any, of relationships so far. What have been the positives? What have you found difficult? What do you think might be the difficulties in future relationships? What do want from a relationship?

There is no 'one-size-fits-all' approach to relationships; all individuals are different. Some general advice includes:

- Never feel rushed into a relationship or enter a relationship just because your friends are, or you feel left out or lonely. A relationship means emotional and lifestyle changes so the time has to be right
- Do not believe that you will only be happy when you meet somebody else; this is a media myth. It can be

- unhelpful to depend on somebody else for your happiness and self-esteem
- Establish some boundaries from the start of a relationship. Be honest about your routines, needs, likes and dislikes
- If your partner is intolerant or unaccepting, consider leaving the relationship; it is unlikely to be positive. A partner needs to understand you and be willing to communicate with you. In return, you also need to be able to accept his or her needs and preferences. You will both have to negotiate solutions and compromise
- Be clear what your boundaries are, especially in relation to physical intimacy. Your partner needs to respect that you might be sensitive to physical touch.
- All relationships are different and develop differently. You might simply start off as good friends.

Sexuality

Sexuality involves the feelings and attractions you experience towards other people. People often consider their sexuality to be either 'heterosexual' (attracted to the opposite sex), 'homosexual' (attracted to people of the same sex) or 'bisexual' (attracted to both sexes), but there are also many other types of sexuality.

Some individuals consider themselves to be 'asexual'. This just means that they do not feel sexually attracted to others; having a sexual relationship is not important to them. They might still, however, enjoy close, emotional relationships with others.

Many young people are unsure about their sexuality identity. It can take a while to work out what feels right. For some people their sexual orientation changes throughout their life. Do not feel pressured or rushed to give yourself a label; it is ok to feel confused.

Being on the autism spectrum might mean you generally feel 'different'; this might impact on your feelings towards your gender and sexuality.

Gender Identity

Gender identity can often be confused with sexuality but the two are not the same. Gender is whether we identify as being a man or a woman. The majority of people identify with the gender they were born, but some identify with the other gender or with none at all.

Further Information

The ChildLine website is aimed at under 19s and has an informative section on 'sexual orientation'. (www.childline.org.uk).

Being Gay Is Ok (www.bgiok.org.uk) contains advice for gay, lesbian and bisexual young people under 25.

Young Stonewall (www.youngstonewall.org.uk) also provides information and support for young lesbian, gay, bisexual and transgender people.

Sex and Intimate Relationships

At some point in a close relationship, partners might decide they would like to have sex. Although the age of consent (the age which you can legally have sex) in the UK is 16, you should only have sex when you feel ready. If you feel pressured into having sex, it is not the right time.

- Sex requires both physical and emotional intimacy; it is important that you feel ready for this
- Many people regret having sex too early and wish they had waited longer
- It is possible to have a satisfying and close relationship without sex; there are many other ways to show love and intimacy

- Never feel pressured into having sex by your partner, and never try to persuade your partner into having sex if s/he does not feel ready
- It is wrong if somebody is pressuring you to have sex or do sexual things you do not want to; this is a form of sexual abuse

If you and your partner decide you are both ready to have intercourse, you will need to ensure you are using a form of contraception to prevent unwanted pregnancies and sexually transmitted diseases.

Free contraception, as well as advice on safe sex, can be obtained from your doctor or from local sexual health services. Many colleges and universities also have drop in services for sexual health matters.

Various types of contraception include condoms (also available to buy from supermarkets and pharmacies) and, for women, the pill, the implant, injections, diaphragms, and emergency contraception (also known as the 'morning after pill'). Discuss with your doctor or nurse which is the most suitable. Remember that some methods of contraception will protect against unwanted pregnancy, but not against sexually transmitted diseases.

Further Information

Further information about safe sex can be obtained from your doctor, or from the following websites.

Brook – the young people's sexual health charity (www.brook.org.uk).

The NHS Sexual Health Hub (www.nhs.org.uk).

The Family Planning Association (www.fpa.org.uk)

Unhealthy relationships

Occasionally people find themselves in an unhealthy relationship with a partner, friend, colleague or even family member. These sorts of unhealthy relationships can include:

- Physical violence or aggression
- Sexual abuse / rape
- Intimidation
- Threats
- Being constantly put down or told you are doing things wrong
- Being blamed for things that are not your fault
- Bullying (including cyberbullying, being deliberately left out, intimidation, name calling, humiliation)
- Being made to feel bad about yourself
- Emotional abuse
- Domestic violence
- Being asked or forced to do things you are uncomfortable with
- Another person attempting to control what you do and where you go

If you are being hurt in any of the above ways, it is important to do something about it straight away. There is never an excuse for anybody to bully, abuse or intimidate another person. What you need to do will differ depending on your situation. Some possibilities include:

Talk to somebody: Talking things through with a trusted friend or family member can help you to consider the situation and what is best to do. Calling ChildLine (for under 19s) or the Samaritans can also be useful; these counsellors are experienced in helping people in these situations and can give you advice and support.

Get support: Various organisations have been set up to support victims of domestic violence (such as 'Women's Aid' and 'Refuge' who run the National Domestic Violence Helpline).

Report it: Bullying, intimidation or abuse in the workplace should be reported to your mentor, line manager, human resources department, or trade union. If you are at school, college or university, speak to a student mentor. Outside of the workplace, serious incidents should be reported to the police.

Leave the situation: If a friendship or relationship has become toxic or uncomfortable, the best thing to do is to walk away. It can seem difficult at first, but various organisations offer help and support.

Activity

You are now about halfway through this book. Perhaps take some time to reflect on the following questions:

About You

What have learned about yourself so far?

What are you improving at?

Which activities are you going to continue doing?

What are you going to find out more about?

About Your Autism

How does autism affect you?

What is your attitude towards your autism? Do you view it as a disability, disorder, difference or advantage?

Is autism a positive or negative in your life, or somewhere in between?

How would you like to view your autism and what difference would that make?

A thoughtful gift you
have received...

A compliment you have
received...

Scribble Page...

An act of kindness you
have received...

An act of kindness you
have performed...

Learning

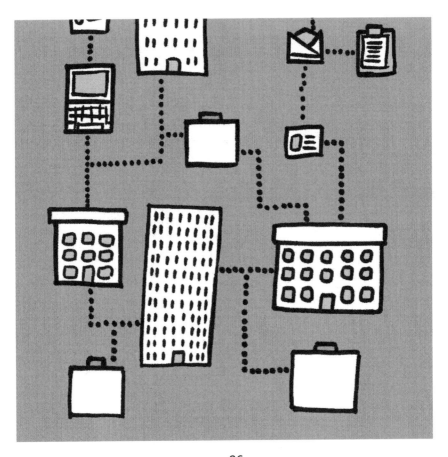

Section 4: Learning

This section covers learning and education – at school, college or university.

> **Activity**
>
> Start with a learning skills self-audit. Read the list of learning skills below. Rate yourself from 1 -5 for each (1= I need more help with this, 5 = I do this very well).
>
> Look at your results. What are your strengths? What support do you need to develop the areas that you find more difficult? If you have a learning mentor, use this list as a starting point for discussion.

Learning Skills

I bring the right equipment and resources.

I listen well and remember what the teacher / tutor has said.

I understand instructions and what I have to do for tasks.

I understand information given out.

I ask questions when I need to.

I participate in group discussions.

I participate in partner work.

I answer questions posed by the teacher / tutor.

I plan my work before I begin it.

I have lots of ideas for different tasks.

I motivate myself to work well independently.

I am confident to give a presentation in front of others.

I can use a computer confidently to present my work.

I can present my ideas in writing.

My work is well-presented.

I can present my ideas through talking and discussion.

I am good at getting started with my work.

I can avoid distractions.

I am good at practical tasks and making things.

I can find the information I need to do my work.

I can use the internet effectively as a research tool.

I check my work thoroughly for mistakes and errors.

I am good at improving my work and acting on feedback.

I revise for tests and exams effectively.

I use effective exam technique.

I complete and hand in all assignments on time.

I am well-organised and know when deadlines and exams are.

These are all useful skills whether you are at school, college, university or doing professional qualifications, and apply regardless of the subjects you are studying.

Autism and learning

Being on the autism spectrum does not necessarily mean you will have difficulties with learning. Just like anybody else, you will have subjects you enjoy and those you do not. There will be some subjects you find easy and some you find harder.

Some individuals on the autism spectrum do also have difficulties with learning, and others may not have difficulty with understanding the topics covered, but might find the learning environment difficult to cope with.

You might, for example, find that sensory sensitivities affect your learning. You might find it impossible to filter out background noise or be overwhelmed by too many visual distractions in the classroom. You might find it easier to study at home or in a library.

Differences in how you communicate and interact with other people might affect your learning. Some courses and classes, for example, require group work or collaborative tasks which can be difficult for some individuals on the autism spectrum. Difficulties in understanding the perspective of others might occasionally lead to misunderstandings with peers or tutors.

Other individuals on the autism spectrum identify having difficulty with some of the following:

- Understanding and interacting with people in positions of authority
- Accepting sometimes things have to be done in a certain way to meet the requirements of the school or examiner
- Having to prove that you know something through producing a set piece of work
- Understanding feedback on work; it can be easy to take criticism personally or not see it in the constructive way it is meant. Teachers and tutors are trying to help their students to improve but sometimes this can seem like they are just pointing out mistakes
- Being a literal thinker and taking instructions and information very literally; you might not always give the information the examiner is looking for
- Rules in some educational establishments might appear inconsistent, causing anxiety. Those on the autism spectrum often prefer rules that make sense and that are applied consistently
- Rewards and sanctions policies for those that do not follow the 'rules' might have been designed for non-autistics. A 'reward' of extra free time or the opportunity

to work with friends, for example, might not motivate everybody
- Feeling anxious when routines change
- Wanting to do everything perfectly; this can cause stress and take up a lot of time
- Preferring to spend extended time focusing on one task, rather than switching quickly between tasks as is often expected

The learning environment

Activity

Consider the list below. Do any of these factors influence your learning negatively? How could you overcome each one?

Sensory issues (e.g. too much background noise, too many distractions, bright lights, smells, loud voices).

The impact of other people (e.g. too many interruptions, anxiety about working in groups, being too close to other people).

Processing time (e.g. needing more time to think about the topic and questions, finding it difficult to move from one activity to the next).

Anxieties in the classroom (e.g. worrying about being asked questions or about what is coming next, anxiety when the routine is changed, worrying if your work is good enough).

Not understanding why some classroom rules exist.

Difficulty with organisation (e.g. bringing the right equipment).

Understanding the task and instructions.

Difficulty taking part in certain activities (e.g. role play, writing from another person's perspective)

Your list will be individual to you. You might only experience some of these difficulties in certain subjects or specific classroom situations. Many things can be improved quite easily. The first step is to identify what has a negative impact on your learning and convey that to your teacher, tutor or mentor. Some schools, colleges and staff might be more 'autism-friendly' than others.

Perhaps you have already considered some ideas that would help you? Some useful strategies might include:

- Changing seating so that you are away from sensory irritations or distractions
- Asking for written versions of the lesson outline or homework task
- Having warning of what is coming up
- Extra time to complete tasks
- Working in a quieter area when appropriate
- Taking on a specific role during group work
- Clear guidelines about how much work and the standard expected
- Support with a specific skill such as understanding different types of question words

Support in education

If you need support with your learning, because of your autism or any other reason, your school, college or university will provide this. Every educational institution is different, but usually there will be a learning support base, or student support services. Here you will find support such as homework / study clubs, extra revision classes, or specialist equipment. Find out what your school, college or university offers and make use of it when you need to. These services are available for all students to make use of; do not feel embarrassed about seeking support. The staff will be experienced in helping students and in liaising with tutors and teachers.

You may have been allocated a key worker or mentor in your school or college to approach if you have any concerns about your learning. Alternatively, your first point of contact could be your form tutor or class teacher. At college or university, find the student support service (or learning support centre) and ask to speak to somebody. They will be able to allocate you a mentor or advisor.

If your school or college considers you have more significant learning needs then you might have been given an 'Education, Health and Care Plan' (EHCP). This is basically a document which outlines the needs you have, what the professionals (such as teachers, social workers or speech and language therapists) need to do to help you, and which educational establishment can best meet your needs. This is your document and you should have a say in what is included. You will be invited to the review meeting each year. When you were younger, your parents or carers probably did most of the talking, but as you become older it is important that you have a bigger say. Make sure your wishes and needs are recorded on the document; once you are 16 you take ownership of the EHCP and have the right to make decisions about what goes in it.

Learning Needs

As well as your autism, you might have been diagnosed with other specific learning needs such as ADHD, dyslexia, dyspraxia, dyscalculia, or speech and language needs. If this applies to you, find out how it affects you (just like you are finding out about your autism), so you can identify any support you may need. There are many strategies which can help you to overcome these differences. Ask your mentor or student support services for more information.

Further Information

British Dyslexia Association (www.bdadyslexia.org.uk) for information about dyslexia and dyscalculia in the workplace and in education.

Dyspraxia Foundation (www.dyspraxiafoundation.org.uk).

Planning and Organisation

Whatever level of education you are in, the hardest part is often getting started! Over the next few pages there are a number of templates[xxv]. You might like to photocopy these or adapt them to meet your specific needs. You might make notes using words, symbols or even small drawings.

The planning board can be used to break down a larger task into smaller steps, and to organise your equipment and time.

The ideas sheet provides space to generate different ideas or ways of completing a task. Weigh up the pros and cons of each before making a final decision.

The essay planner is a frame to plan what to include in a longer written task. Jot down the key points in each section and then build your essay around them.

A to-do list is a useful way of remembering everything you need to do. The act of writing it all down and ticking each task off once complete can reduce worry.

The homework planners and revision planners can be used to prioritise the tasks you need to do. Try to be specific. Rather than writing 'Revise science', state exactly what you will do ('Watch a revision video on photosynthesis and complete a past exam question'). Add a deadline for each task and to tick each off once complete. Try to start the tasks as soon as you can so that you do not have a last minute panic!

Planning Board

My task is:			Date due:
Steps I need to take:	**Equipment / support needed:**	**By when / How long:**	**Done:**

Ideas Sheet

Ideas	Pros	Cons

I have decided to choose idea …. because…

Essay Planner

Title / Question
Introduction (A good introduction will explain what the topic of your essay is and give a brief background to the topic):
Arguments for:
Arguments against:
Conclusion (A good conclusion summarises the main points made in your essay and comes to a conclusion or answer to the initial question):

To Do List

To-Do List!

To Do: By When: Done:

Homework Planner

Subject:	Task:	Due date:	Done:

Revision Planner

Topics to revise	Revision strategies to use (e.g. testing myself, doing a past paper)	By when	Done?

Giving presentations

In school and college, you might be asked to give a presentation in front of your classmates. Presentation skills are useful to develop. There are times at college, university, in the workplace, or in everyday life when it is necessary to speak in front of other people. In school, giving presentations is a chance to show your knowledge and share your ideas with other people. Some people find giving presentations scary, but the good news is that everybody can learn and improve their presentation skills.

Activity

What makes a good presentation? Think back to the last presentation or talk you heard. What made it effective?

Your list might have included:

- ✓ I could hear the speaker.
- ✓ I understood what the speaker was talking about.
- ✓ The speaker was interesting.
- ✓ There was a clear introduction so that I knew what was coming up.
- ✓ The presentation was well structured – it made sense.
- ✓ The speaker spoke about things that were relevant.
- ✓ If there was a PowerPoint, I could read the writing on the slides.
- ✓ Pictures were relevant and interesting.
- ✓ There was an effective ending.
- ✓ The speaker gave enough detail.

Reducing anxiety

Many people feel nervous before giving a presentation. Your mouth might go dry, you might need to use the toilet or feel you have 'butterflies' in your tummy. You might feel you have forgotten everything you were about to say! Don't worry; there are plenty of things you can do to combat this:

- Practise your presentation and get feedback. If you have practised, you are less likely to forget it and will feel more confident.
- Take cue cards or notes so that you can read from them if you do forget what you want to say.
- Have a bottle of water with you and go to the toilet before the lesson.
- Take some long, slow, deep breaths before your presentation. This helps you feel calmer and more relaxed.
- Praise yourself – not everybody manages to stand in front of people, so very well done if you have achieved this!
- Remember you will not get it perfect the first time. Every time you give a presentation you will feel less nervous and improve a bit more.
- Check with your teacher or tutor if you could build up your skills slowly – perhaps you could stand up with a partner the first time if that helps you to feel more confident?

Activity

If you have to give a presentation, plan it in advance. Include these headings on your plan or spider diagram and add some detail to each one.

Introduction (What are you going to say to introduce the topic? You need to tell your audience what you will talk about and the points you are going to cover.)

Main points (Make notes of the points you will cover.)

Conclusion (How will you summarise what you have said and come to a conclusion?)

Visuals If you are using a PowerPoint, check:

• Your slides are structured in the right order.

- Your writing is big enough for the audience to see.

- Your writing is clear and can be seen on the background.

- You put only the main points on the slides and don't just read the slides aloud. Talk about each point in more detail.

- Pictures or video links are clear and relevant.

Props. Do you need any other props or objects to show to the audience?

Cue cards. Are you going to make small cue cards or notes to refer to when you are speaking?

Practising your presentation is important to feel prepared. Ask a friend, family member or other trusted adult to watch you practise and ask them to answer the questions below. Alternatively, record yourself and watch it back, answering the questions about your own performance.

Did I:

speak loudly enough?

speak slowly and clearly so that everybody could understand?

vary my voice and intonation to make my speech more interesting?

look at the audience and not just my notes?

stand still so as not to distract the audience?

use gesture and facial expression appropriately to add to my points?

explain any complex words or new ideas that the audience might not know?

keep to the topic?

give enough detail so that the audience understood, but not too much to bore them?

have a clear introduction?

make my points in a sensible order?

have a clear ending?

refer to any pictures or props?

have a clear PowerPoint that could be understood?

Revision, tests and exams

At some point you will have to complete tests or exams. Some might be relatively informal tests in class at the end of each topic to enable your tutors to see how you are getting on, while others might be formal examinations going towards qualifications. Exams can be stressful, mainly because people want to do their best and are worried about the outcome.

Even outside of your educational career, you might not be able to avoid tests and exams. Many people want to drive a car one day – for this you need to pass a theory test, a hazard perception test and a practical driving test. When looking for employment, you might be asked to complete a written test at a job interview. Some jobs and careers require you to pass tests once you have got the job in order to qualify for promotion.

Why do we need exams?

Tests and exams have a range of functions. Sometimes you will have tests in class so your teachers can see what you have understood and what they need to do to help you progress further. More formal exams (such as GCSEs and A levels) are used to show your ability in different subjects; this can help colleges and employers see what you are good at. Other exams help to ensure safety and high standards. We have to pass a driving test, for example, to prove that we are a safe driver.

Doctors and surgeons have to pass exams to prove that they have the knowledge to be able to treat people quickly and in the best way.

What's so scary about exams?

Taking tests and exams can be a stressful situation for lots of people. Many people worry they have not learned enough or they will forget everything or run out of time or just not know the answers. Some people become overwhelmed in an exam situation and become so nervous that their mind goes 'blank' and they cannot remember what they have learned. Others may be perfectionists who worry so much about answering the first question perfectly they run out of time to answer other questions! Other people, however, love exams! Some people enjoy having the chance to show what they have learned and to find out what they need to do to improve even further.

Activity

Reflect on your experience of tests and exams so far. What has gone well? What would you like to improve at?

Learning effective revision strategies and exam techniques can help you to feel prepared and get the best results you can.

Support in tests and examinations

If you meet certain criteria, your school, college or university might assess you for additional support. You will usually be asked to complete some tests. You might be eligible for a reader (somebody to read questions to you), a scribe (somebody to write down what you say), use of voice-text software, or extra time in exams. If this applies to you, make sure you are aware of what you can expect and learn how to use these concessions effectively. Student support services should offer you advice on how to use this support most effectively.

What should I expect on exam day?

Once you know what to expect, exams aren't so scary. Usually you will take your exam in a large room or hall and be told which desk to sit at. Usually the teacher in charge will seat pupils alphabetically. Some students are able to take their exam in an individual room if they have specific learning needs – you should check with your teacher if this applies to you.

Make sure you have everything that you will need. Once the exam starts, you are not allowed to leave the room to go and get things. Do not take in any papers or notes as this will be seen as cheating.

Mobile phones are not allowed in exams or tests as they disturb others and students could use them to find out the answers on the Internet or by texting someone. Make sure you turn your mobile phone off and leave it at home or in your bag outside the examination hall. Most schools will have lockers or a place where you can leave your bags when you are in the examination hall.

You will usually start by filling in the front page of the exam paper. This might ask for your name, date of birth, candidate number and school's 'centre' number. The invigilator will tell you the school number, and it should also be displayed in the room. You can be told your candidate number if you have forgotten it.

'Exam conditions' begin when you enter the examination room and end when you leave. Exam conditions mean that you are not allowed to talk to other students. If you do so, the invigilator will assume you are cheating and you will both be disqualified from your exams. If another student tries to talk to you during the exam, ignore them. If you have a problem, or are feeling unwell, raise your hand, remain in your seat and wait for the invigilator to come and speak to you. Don't call out because this will disturb other students. If you need to borrow equipment, raise your hand and speak to the invigilator. Trying to ask a friend may result in you both being disqualified for cheating.

What if I do really badly?

Try not to worry if you think you haven't done as well on an exam as you had hoped. You will often have to wait a few weeks or months before you receive the results and worrying during that time will not change your result. It is usual to feel you have done badly. Usually people find they have done better than they expected. Many subjects are made up of exams as well as controlled assessments or coursework, so your final result will be an average of these things.

If you haven't done as well as you had hoped, there are plenty of options. Some people find they are still able to pursue their chosen college course or employment route even if their results were slightly lower than expected. Many colleges offer the option to retake exams, alongside your chosen course of study. This can be a good opportunity to have another go and improve your grade. Other students might choose to retake the subject at an evening class or through distance learning. There are always other options available, and you should discuss what would be best for you with a careers advisor at your school or college.

Revision

Revision simply means revisiting the work we have covered in lessons so that it is fresher in our minds for the exam. We learn best by revising actively rather than passively. Some 'active' revision ideas include:

Doing past exam questions and comparing your answers to the marking scheme

Making a mind map or spider diagram of the topic

Testing yourself on a topic

Asking another person to test you on a topic

Explaining a topic to somebody else and answering questions on it

Teaching somebody else a topic

Doing online revision tests and activities

Watching a video clip about the topic

Making a presentation about the topic to other people

Making a poster about a topic

Reading over your notes, annotating and highlighting key points

Reorganising and summarising notes from lessons

Making and playing a game or quiz about the topic

Practising doing timed essays or questions in preparation for the exam

Discussing a topic with other people, revising the same thing and questioning each other

Using revision guides and study guides

Activity

How do you usually revise? Is it effective? Try some of the ideas listed above to make your revision more 'active'.

Is it worthwhile making a revision timetable. Find out from your tutor the topics that you will be tested on. Decide when you will revise each topic and how you will revise the topic. Plan this in advance so that you only have to do a small amount of revision each day rather than trying to cram everything in at the last minute.

Effective exam technique

- You will feel more confident and relaxed if you have prepared well. Begin revision early and revise in frequent, short sessions. Use active revision techniques to engage with the content and do past practice papers so you know what to expect

- Use the exam checklist on the next page to make sure you know exactly where and when the exam is and that you have the right equipment
- Try to have a good night's sleep the night before and eat a healthy breakfast in the morning
- Read the instructions and questions carefully before you begin. Check which questions you need to answer. On some tests you have to answer all of them; on others there may be a choice (*'Answer either question 1 or question 2'*)
- Plan how you will use your time. You should spend longer on questions worth the most marks
- The amount of marks that are available will indicate how much detail you need to give in your answer. If the question is only worth one mark, you will not be expected to write a whole page
- Write as legibly as you can so that your work can be read
- Whatever the subject, remember to use clear spelling, punctuation and grammar
- If you make a mistake, put a neat line through it and write your new answer in
- Show all your working out in subjects like Maths and Science – you get extra marks for this
- For longer essay questions, plan your answer out in a few short bullet points before you begin
- If you are really stuck on a question, don't spend too long worrying about it. Go on to the next question and return to the tricky question if you have time at the end
- If you finish early, use the time to check over your answer. Have you answered the question accurately? Have you included enough detail? Have you checked your calculations?

Moving on

Let's consider now choosing the next steps in your educational career. Deciding if and what you would like to study at college or university might seem a big decision.

Studying at college or university is an exciting opportunity. You can choose subjects you enjoy and pursue these in more depth. You have more freedom than at school, often no longer having to wear a uniform and having more control of your own time. College and university is a great opportunity to meet new friends and get to know like-minded people with similar interests. Many courses also contain vocational elements which means they are directly related to a job you might like to do afterwards. Let's consider some of your options:

Sixth form college. A sixth form college usually takes students for two years (age 16–18) with the focus on A-levels, although a range of other courses may be available.

Further education college. A further education college often takes students predominantly between the ages of 16 and 19. Usually a range of part-time and full-time courses is on offer in a range of subject areas, academic and vocational. Colleges often also cater for adult learners, and many also offer courses during the evenings.

University. A university is where you study for degrees or higher degrees. Students usually attend for three or four years, depending on the course. Courses have different entry requirements, some requiring specific grades at A-levels, others accepting a wider range of previous qualifications. Some degrees have a work placement or study abroad built in. Some courses qualify you to enter a profession, while other professions require further qualifications at a postgraduate level.

Distance learning. Studying via distance learning means you do most of your studying at home in your own time. The Open University is known for its distance learning courses, although some other universities also offer distance-learning courses. You will be sent materials to study, and will have access to a virtual learning space. You might have to attend some face-to-face or online tutorials. To do well through distance learning you will need to be able to motivate yourself and manage your own time well. This mode of study suits people who enjoy studying alone and teaching themselves. It can also suit those who want to work and study simultaneously.

Evening classes. Some colleges, universities, schools, libraries and community centres offer courses in the evenings or at weekends. These are often aimed at adults who want to continue learning. Typical subjects on offer include foreign languages, maths, English, art and crafts, childcare, mechanics, accounting and basic skills, although there can also be a wide range of options. Evening classes can be a good way of trying out something new while you continue working or studying. It can enable you to try a new subject without having to give up work or before you decide on a longer term commitment. Evening classes can be a way of pursuing a hobby further and meeting like-minded people.

Apprenticeships. During an apprenticeship you work and study for a related qualification at the same time. You are paid a wage while you are doing an apprenticeship. A range of apprenticeships are available at different levels.

Other options. The range of options and opportunities on offer is constantly changing and differs from one area to another. A good starting point is to make an appointment with your school or college careers advisor and ask what possibilities there are in your local area.

Further Information

Activities in the 'Employment' section of this book might help you to decide which career path you might be best suited for.

You might also find some of the following websites useful:

www.ucas.com – Universities and Colleges Admissions Service (UCAS) website for information and how to apply for undergraduate courses at university.

www.open.ac.uk – The Open University.

www.prospects.ac.uk – Website with search directory of postgraduate courses and careers options.

www.thecompleteuniversityguide.co.uk – Website containing information about university life.

www.nationalcareersservice.direct.gov.uk– National Careers Service (careers and job advice with a specific section for 13–19-year-olds).

www.findapprenticeship.service.gov.uk – Apprenticeship service in England.

www.futurelearn.co.uk – free online short courses in a range of subjects. These do not lead to qualifications but can be a useful way of trying out different subject areas and distance learning.

www.notgoingtouni.co.uk – site dedicated to apprenticeships, gap years, distance learning and jobs.

Moving on to college or university

Studying at college or university is different to school. You will be expected to learn more independently, organise your own time and take more responsibility for yourself. It can also be a wonderful opportunity to meet people with similar interests and learn lots of new skills. Deciding which college or university to attend can be a big decision. Take your time and research your options fully.

Activity

Once you have decided on the course you would like to study, make a list of the colleges or universities you would consider attending which offer that course. Find out when these institutions have open days and plan to attend these. Make a list of questions you would like to ask at the open day. You might need to know:

How long is the course? How many hours per week?

How is the course assessed?

Is there a practical element or work experience?

Do you have a choice of modules?

What are the options once you have finished the course?

What are the college / university facilities like?

After your visits, make a list of the pros and cons of each college or university. Think about the course, location, travel, living arrangements, finances, support available and anything else that might be relevant to you.

University

If you choose to go to university, you will probably have more to consider than simply the courses available. You might also have to consider whether or not you want to move away from home. Living independently for the first time can be a great experience, but there are also a big learning curve.

Activity

If you are considering moving away to university, make a list of what you consider to be the advantages and disadvantages of moving away and continuing to live at home. How could you overcome some of the disadvantages on your list?

Some of the advantages might have included:

The opportunity to live independently and have more control over your life.

A chance to feel more like an adult.

The opportunity to live with people of a similar age and with similar interests.

Living closer to the university and therefore eliminating travel costs.

Being able to get more involved in student life.

And some of the disadvantages might have included:

The financial cost of living away.

Leaving your family, home, friends and life you are used to.

Concerns about living with other people or not enjoying typical 'student life'.

Your list is likely to be very personal to you, and only you can make the final decision.

There are other issues to take into account when you are thinking about going to university. Not only do you have to consider which course and university is most suitable, but also the financial implications of higher education. To study at university you will have to pay tuition fees and, especially if you choose to live away from home, you will also have living expenses (e.g. your accommodation, bills and food). Most students take out a student loan which they then begin to pay back once they are earning over a certain amount. Tuition fees and student loans differ from university to university and from one geographic region to another so look on your university's website, as well as on the UCAS and Student Finance websites to find out the most up-to-date information. Remember there are often grants and bursaries available that can help with the cost of further education. Again, check with your university to see what you could be eligible for.

If you are considering living away from home, more information about budgeting and independent living skills in section 6 of this book.

Beginning at college or university

Once you have decided on your course and college or university, there is a lot of planning to do. Your college or university will usually provide an induction pack or host an induction day. This is when you will receive your timetable and other useful information about the course. If you are living away from home, there will be special events to help you get to know the new area and university. Make the most of opportunities on offer; there might be tours of the university or library, a freshers' fair for you to sign up to different clubs and activities, or other welcome events.

Activity

Make a list of the things you need to find out before you begin your course and during your first week at university. See if you can find the answers to any of them from the university website or information you have been sent. For any other questions, make sure you ask you tutor, mentor, fellow students or student support services in the first few days.

It is fine not to go to university if you do not want to, or to take a 'gap year' before beginning your studies. Some young people decide to gain experience of the job market first or want to take more time to make a decision. There is always the option to go to university later on as a mature student.

Your favourite childhood film…

A piece of wisdom you have received…

Scribble Page…

Your favourite childhood book…

The time of day you are at your best…

Employment

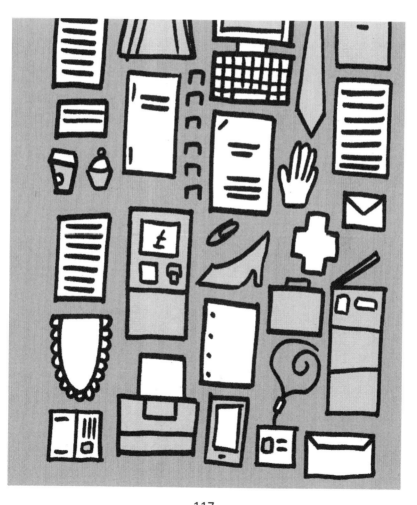

Section 5: Employment

In this chapter you will find information about deciding what sort of work you would like to do, applying for jobs, and thriving in the workplace.

Thinking about jobs and employment when you are young can be quite scary. Maybe you have absolutely no idea what you would like to do or which job you would be best suited for. It could be that you have not enjoyed work experience or part-time employment so are uncertain about the world of work. Maybe you are not sure where to start – how do you find and apply for a job? Or perhaps you are worried about doing a job, fitting in in the workplace or finding something you enjoy?

Deciding on a career path

You are trying to decide what to do for a job or career. Where do you begin? You might not be able to decide between a few things you are interested in, or you might know roughly what you are interested in (education, health, ICT) but not know which role you are best suited for. You might have no idea at all!

Let's consider first why people work: [xxvi]

- to earn money to live

- to be able to spend time doing something they enjoy

- to learn new things

- to make a contribution to society or to make a difference

- to help others

- to meet new people

Some people work for a combination of these reasons or for different reasons at different times. When you are a student, for example, you might get a job to earn extra money for a holiday or for driving lessons. You might not mind too much what the job is, as it might only be short-term and something to fit around your studies. When you are older, however, and looking for full-time work, however, it might be more important to find something more meaningful to you. There is also evidence that having a job makes us happier; people who work feel more valued and confident.

All of us have a different 'ideal' job. What will suit one person will not suit another; we all have different likes, dislikes and interests.

When deciding what you would like to do, you need to take into consideration:

• What are you interested in and what tasks do you enjoy doing?

• What sort of environment would you prefer to work in – indoors, outdoors, office, school, hospital, with others, busy environment, quiet environment, with animals, with children, with elderly people, with customers …?

• Do you prefer working with others or independently?

• What qualifications do you have, and are you willing to study for further qualifications that some jobs require?

• Do you want to work shifts, nights, or a regular nine to five?

• Would you be willing to wear a uniform?

• Do you want a job that you can forget about in our free time or a job that requires you to do extra work when you get home?

• Do you want a job where you can progress up the career ladder and take on more responsibility?

• Do you want to learn new skills?

• Do you want a job where you can be creative?

Being on the autism spectrum does not prevent you from working. Individuals on the autism spectrum work successfully in a wide range of jobs and professions, from science to the arts, from computing to caring professions. Consider your personal strengths, interests and values to discover what you suit you best. Some individuals on the autism spectrum find they excel in jobs such as nursing, teaching or other roles. Do not be led by stereotypes such as that those on the autism spectrum all want to work alone on computers all day. Every individual is different.

Further Information

The Prospects website has a free online quiz which suggests jobs you might be suited for based on your answers (www.prospects.ac.uk).

Things to remember:

• Some jobs require certain qualifications or experience before you begin. In other roles, you can gain qualifications while you are working and be trained on the job.

• You do not have to get it right the first time. Many people change jobs or careers once they have tried something out. You might need to try a few things before finding what you enjoy most.

• You might not find the perfect job at once, but whatever your role, you can often learn new skills and experiences that will help you move into your ideal position at a later date.

There are lots of options for work. Here are a few options:

(a) Looking for a job the traditional way and becoming employed by another person or company.

(b) Self-employment - working for yourself or having your own business (e.g. your own gardening company or your own cafe).

(c) Working freelance - taking on projects for different people at different times (many people in the creative industries work on a freelance basis).

(d) Doing an apprenticeship - learning on the job and having some time in the week to gain a related qualification.

(e) Some people choose to work part-time and study part-time.

Activity

Answer the following questions in your journal:

What are you good at? (Your skills, strengths, qualifications and hobbies)

What are you interested in? (Consider your values, interests, hobbies and college / university subjects)

What sort of physical environment would you like to work in?

Which activities give you energy? Which drain your energy?

What does work mean to you? What do you want to get from work?

How would you like to be remembered?

Think about your strengths and skills. Individuals on the autism spectrum have a wide range of strengths which they can bring to the workplace. Perhaps some of these apply to you?

Creative thinker	Methodical
Logical thinker	Attention to detail
Problem solver	Innovative

Unique	Independent worker
Reliable	Conscientious
Intense focus	In-depth knowledge

Now you have thought about what you want from the world of work, think next about which roles you might be best suited for.

- A good place to begin is your school, college or university careers service. They will be able to offer you advice, information and guidance about various careers.
- Doing work experience or shadowing people in different roles can be a great way of trying out different jobs and getting an insight into how the workplace works. Sometimes work experience opportunities are available through your college or university, or you may be able to arrange your own by asking family, neighbours or relatives if you could shadow them for a day or two in their workplace.
- A part-time job while you are at college or university can be a good way of learning what you enjoy and learning about different roles.
- Prospects (www.prospects.ac.uk) is a useful website which contains information about job roles and careers. There is information about the qualifications required, training routes and working conditions.

Activity

Make notes about the information you find out. Are there any roles you would be interested in? Make plans to investigate these further. Could you do any job shadowing? Which qualifications would you need for the role?

Your autism

Individuals on the autism spectrum are found in a variety of job roles, just like other people. Having autism will not stop you from working or getting a job you enjoy. Indeed, many find that they enjoy the routine and purpose of the workplace. You might, however, need to consider some of the following things:

Do you have any sensory issues that could affect you in the workplace? If you do, what coping strategies could you put into place to help you?

Do you find it difficult to work in a busy environment, or do you feel exhausted after being around people? If so, you might consider roles where there is more opportunity for independent working or working in a quieter environment.

Do you find it difficult to plan and organise your time? What difficulties could there be in the workplace, and what strategies could you use to help you cope with these?

How do you communicate with others? What support will you need with this?

How well do you cope with change and learning new things?

How do you react to authority? Do you like to be told what to do? How do you respond to feedback and criticism?

Activity

Consider the questions above. If you have any worries, discuss them with your careers' advisor, mentor, friend or relative. Many of the autism organisations listed in section 1 of this book also offer support with employment. Contact your nearest organisation. See what they offer and if this could help you.

The 'Access To Work' scheme in the UK also provides support for employees with disabilities and differences such as autism spectrum conditions.

Disclosing your autism

Whether you tell anyone about your autism is a matter of personal preference. Under current UK legislation, you can tell an employer about a disability (and autism is classed as a 'disability' for this purpose) at any point, before, during or after the recruitment process. It is very much a personal preference if and when you decide to tell your employer about your autism. If you do tell your employer, it is their responsibility to keep it confidential and not tell your colleagues, unless you want them to. You only <u>have</u> to tell an employer about a disability if it will put your health and safety or the health and safety of others at risk.

Possible reasons to disclose:

• You will not have to be as concerned with concealing stimming, sensory sensitivities or social confusions that are part of your autism, as those who know will realise these are often autistic traits.

• Employers might be more supportive and understanding if there are certain tasks you find more challenging or need extra support with.

• You might not be entitled to workplace support until you have disclosed your autism. Without having some knowledge of autism, others might struggle to help you meet your needs.

• You might need 'reasonable adjustments' in the workplace under the Equality Act (2010). You can only request these once you have disclosed your autism. A reasonable adjustment is something that employers can do to ensure that disabled employees (including those on the autism spectrum) are not put at a disadvantage compared to their colleagues.

• Colleagues might be more understanding that you socialise and develop friendships in different ways.

• You might feel more comfortable knowing that your employer and colleagues are aware of your autism.

Risks involved with disclosing:

• You might feel more comfortable if the people you work with do not know you have autism.

• You might meet with prejudices or stereotypes. Some people are not very informed about autism and might assume that you have certain traits or difficulties or are unable to do a job. Disclosure is no absolute guarantee of accommodation or understanding. However, the Equality Act (2010) makes it unlawful to discriminate against somebody because of a disability.

• You might not want to feel that you are different or getting any different treatment.

• You might be worried that knowing you have autism will prevent some employers from offering you a job.

• If you have developed successful coping strategies, others may not immediately recognise your difficulties and may assume that you are making excuses for unacceptable behaviour or trying to avoid certain aspects of a role.

You might choose not to disclose that you have autism and that is fine too. It might not be important to you, or you might feel that it does not affect you in your particular workplace.

Activity

Have you considered whether or not you want to tell the people you work with about your autism? What might be the advantages and disadvantages?

How to disclose

Decide when is the most appropriate time (on an application form, before an interview, during an interview, after being offered a job). This is very much personal preference and depends on how your autism affects you.

You might feel comfortable speaking to your employer alone or might prefer to ask a support worker to accompany you. You might wish to write down the important points and what helps you in certain situations.

Focus on the positives. It is not helpful to your employer to present a long list of things you cannot do. What your employer will want to hear are the proactive steps you have taken to help you overcome any difficulties or differences. They will want to see that you have a good level of awareness about how your autism affects you and that you have a positive attitude to what you can achieve. Here are some examples:

> *'My autism means that I sometimes have difficulty in processing detailed oral instructions. However, I make sure that I always carry a notepad to write down the important points so that I don't forget anything, and I always ask if I feel I need things repeating.'*

> *'I wear earplugs so that I am not distracted by noise in the environment. This helps me to concentrate on my work.'*

Further Information

Your employer or managers might want to learn more about autism in the workplace, or want support with how they can best support you. There is information on the National Autistic Society website; employers can also receive support from local autism organisations and the Access to Work scheme.

Finding job advertisements

The first step in the job application process is finding out which jobs are available. Jobs are advertised in different places. Often, job adverts are found online on various job websites. There are specific websites that advertise jobs in different industries (e.g. the TES website for jobs in education, the Law Gazette website for jobs in the legal sector) and many companies advertise their vacancies on their website. Newspapers and magazines sometimes also contain job adverts. You can visit your local job centre which can help you find jobs or look on Universal Jobsearch (www.gov.uk/jobsearch).

Once you have found a job you might like to apply for, you need to find out more information. Often more information is available online, or you can email or phone the employer. Things you might need to find out at this stage are:

• The location of the job: Would you be able to get there easily?

• The level of the job: Is it at the level you are looking for? Do you have the qualifications and experience necessary to apply?

• Is it full-time or part-time: How many hours per week and what is the shift pattern?

• The job role: What tasks are involved?

If you feel you are suited to the job and it meets your requirements, then it is time to complete the next step: filling in the application form.

Applying for jobs

The next step in the process is usually filling in an application form. This allows the employer to see the main details of all of the applicants who are interested and to shortlist them. The application form allows employers to see quickly if the applicants have the right qualifications and experiences to do the job, enables employers to pick the best candidates to invite for an interview, and gives the applicants an opportunity to write about their skills, experiences and why they would be suited for the job.

Whatever the job, all employers will be looking for some of the same things on the application form: neat presentation showing that you have taken care with the application; information presented clearly so that it is easy to pick out; all of the questions answered showing that you can follow the instructions that were given; good spelling, punctuation and grammar showing that you can communicate clearly; a clear summary of why you are applying for the job and how your previous skills and experiences make you suited for the job.

It is also important to make sure that you send the application before the deadline as applications received after that date will not be considered.

Job applications take a lot of practice and different employers look for different things. Employers will look at all of the applications and choose the best to invite for an interview. If you are successful, they will contact you with the details of the interview.

> **Activity**
>
> Ask your careers' advisor, mentor or a family member to check over your application form before you submit it. It can help to have another person to check for typos and errors and to support you in answering the questions correctly.

The job interview

Congratulations, you have been successful in getting a job interview! Getting a job interview is a great achievement; your application form and CV (résumé) have impressed the employer, and they believe you have the necessary qualifications, skills and experiences to be able to do the job. Well done! But now comes the scary part – attending an interview. Most people get nervous and anxious about attending an interview; this is perfectly normal – you want to show yourself in the best possible light, only have a short time to impress the employer, are in direct competition with other applicants and are not quite sure what to expect. Good news is that there are many strategies and techniques you can use to overcome nerves and prepare well for an interview.

The purpose of interviews

Interviews are opportunities for employers to learn more about applicants and decide who would be the best person for the job. Employers will have already made a shortlist from the written applications they have received. However, many candidates will appear similar on paper, with the same sort of qualifications and experiences. Interviews serve several purposes: an opportunity to meet candidates and ask more detailed questions about their experiences, skills and motivation for applying; a chance to find out more about candidates' personal qualities and characteristics (e.g. are they enthusiastic, willing to learn, able to relate to customers?) and an opportunity to ask candidates to complete a task which will give them more information about their ability to do the job. Interviews are also opportunities for applicants to find out more about the job and company. It is a two-way process to help both sides decide if this would be the best fit.

Before you go to the interview

• Whatever the job, all employers are looking for employees who are reliable, responsible and punctual. It is important to be on time for your interview, so plan your journey in advance. Make sure you know where you are going, how you will get there and how long it will take. Do a 'trial run' if you have chance.

• A smart, clean and tidy appearance shows that you are taking the interview seriously. A smart shirt or blouse and trousers or skirt or a dress is usually appropriate. Wear smart shoes, not trainers or flip-flops. Some workplaces will expect you to wear a skirt or trouser suit. Keep your make-up discreet and take care of your personal hygiene. It is most important to feel comfortable in what you are wearing as this will help you to relax. Try your outfit on before the interview.

• Check what you need to take with you. Some employers might ask you to take your examination certificates, a portfolio of work or your ID.

At the interview

• You will usually have to report to the reception. Smile, speak clearly and look in the direction of the person you are speaking to. This gives a good impression. 'Good morning. My name is … . I'm here for an interview for the position of … .'

• You will usually be asked to take a seat and wait until it is your turn.

• When the interviewer comes to meet you, it is usual to introduce yourself and give a firm handshake.

• You might be interviewed by an individual or a panel of several people. They will ask you questions about your previous experiences and why you want the job. This is your opportunity to tell the employer about yourself in more detail.

• You might be asked to complete a task such as give a presentation, complete a written task, present a portfolio or work on a group task. You will be told in advance if this is expected.

• You will also have the opportunity to ask any questions you might have about the role.

After the interview

• The interviewer will tell you when you can expect to hear whether you have been successful or not. Some might make a decision that day; others may take a week or so before they decide.

• Many interviewers will give you feedback on your interview. This is a good opportunity to find out what you did well and what you can improve on for the next time.

Activity

Your college or university careers service may offer the opportunity to attend a 'mock interview'. This is an opportunity to practise your interview skills and receive some feedback from people who want to help you. You could also try practising with a friend or family member.

There are also often free online courses available on Future Learn (www.futurelearn.com) and other sites about various employment skills such as filling in applications, interview skills and presentation skills.

Sometimes, individuals on the autism spectrum can find job interviews difficult. Do any of the following apply to you?

- Finding eye contact uncomfortable or finding appropriate facial expression difficult, meaning you may come across as nervous, lacking confidence or disinterested
- Unusual body language. Some individuals on the autism spectrum can 'stim' (make repetitive movements such as hand flapping) when nervous or anxious
- Some individuals on the autism spectrum report that they have particularly quiet or loud voices; others may find it difficult to vary their intonation and add expression
- Difficulties engaging in 'small talk' or 'social chit-chat' which make up an informal part of the interview
- Intense anxiety or nervousness and not knowing how to cope with this
- Giving too much or too little information – assuming that a potential employer already knows or does not know certain information
- Uncertainty about which information is important and relevant
- Talking out of turn or appearing to interrupt
- Embarrassment about having to 'sell' yourself and talk about your good points
- Misinterpreting questions or being unsure about what the interviewer is looking for
- Difficulty answering questions in which you are required to imagine a 'hypothetical' scenario

- Difficulties contributing to a group discussion.
- Directness or honesty which means you might not give answers which the interviewer is looking for
- Difficulties in 'putting yourself in the employer's shoes'. You might find it difficult to identify what you can bring to the team or employer
- A lack of previous experiences to reflect on
- Low self-esteem and a lack of self-belief
- Sensory issues (such as sensitivity to light, noise, physical proximity) which can increase discomfort and anxiety (and therefore have a negative impact on performance) in the interview situation
- Executive functioning difficulties affecting planning and preparing for the interview

Activity

The good news is that you can learn to overcome any of these difficulties with practice! The first step is simply becoming aware of them. Make a note of which affect you and what you think you could do. Then discuss your concerns with your careers advisor or mentor. Again, a practise, or 'mock', interview can really help here.

First days on the job

The first day in a new job can be a strange experience! Everybody else already seems to know what to do and may appear too busy to help you. However, it is also the perfect time to ask questions and find out how everything works.

Things you may need to find out before or during your first day:

- What the dress code is
- What time you start and finish work
- Where you have to sign in and out
- Where the toilets and staff room are
- Where you can leave your valuables

- What the arrangements are for break and lunch times
- What the tea and coffee arrangements are (e.g. in some workplaces people bring their own, in others there may be a kitty system in place)
- If you need a computer log-in
- How to use the photocopier, printer or other equipment
- What to do in case of fire
- Any other health and safety regulations
- The tasks you are expected to do

Larger organisations usually provide workplace information in the form of a written welcome pack, but in other places you will have to ask your manager or colleagues.

Activity

Open-plan offices are now the norm but can present many challenges for those on the autism spectrum: background noise, constant movement, frequent interruptions, the expectation of multi-tasking, feeling you are being observed by others, having to socialise as you work …. If you find yourself working in such an environment consider some of the challenges it may present and how you could overcome them.

In the workplace

The first few weeks in any new job can be quite confusing and overwhelming as there is a lot to learn. However, this is perfectly normal! Make sure you ask about things you are unsure of and make notes about things you need to remember. Ask your line manager for feedback about how things are going and if there is anything you need to work on.

Activity

Reflect on your experiences of work so far, including any work experience, part-time jobs or voluntary work. What has gone well? What have you enjoyed? Have there been any difficulties?

Some individuals on the autism spectrum experience some difficulties in the workplace. Often these difficulties are not necessarily to do with the job, but with communicating with colleagues or with understanding the 'unwritten' rules in the workplace. Some examples of difficulties experienced by those on the autism spectrum are:

- getting on with colleagues
- feeling bullied or left out by colleagues
- needing or wanting to spend break times alone rather than with colleagues
- not understanding 'office politics'
- a lack of tolerance from colleagues or managers
- difficulties communicating their needs
- environmental issues (e.g. the sensory and social implications of the 'open-plan office')
- preferring routine and structure; perhaps being thought of as inflexible
- preferring to work independently, rather than with others
- misinterpreting instructions or other people's behaviours
- differences in the way they respond to people in positions of authority

These things, however, do not always apply to everybody. Often it is just a case of finding the right workplace environment and group of colleagues for you. The better that you are able to reflect on your autism and any differences, the easier this may be. As you become more assertive and confident, it will become easier to communicate your needs and concerns. You will also learn from experience about which environments and tasks suit you best. Remember too, that autism support organisations can be very helpful in providing workplace mentors and useful advice.

Some general tips for thriving in the workplace:

- Make the most of your induction period. You may be given a mentor or the opportunity to shadow more experienced colleagues. This is an excellent time to ask questions that you may have about the job.
- Do not allow concerns or worries to build up. Ask about things you are unsure of.
- Ask for feedback on your performance.
- Make the most of any training or development opportunities that are on offer and keep up-to-date with the latest developments in your field.
- Follow your workplace protocols with regards to health and safety, customer service and other expected standards.
- Be honest about how your autism affects you. You might not wish to discuss this with all of your colleagues but it can be helpful to discuss it with your line manager, mentor or human resources department.
- Be pro-active in coming up with ideas and solutions that could help you in the workplace.
- It is fine not to socialise with your colleagues outside of work if you do not wish to; just be polite, assertive and thank them for inviting you.
- Pay attention to the little things in the workplace which can cause friction or tension between colleagues. It is often little things like not taking turns to make hot drinks, or leaving equipment in the wrong place which can cause upset.

Activity

If you have had negative work experiences, do not let it put you off from applying or future jobs. Reflect carefully on why the job did not turn out well and what you could do differently next time. Remember you might have simply been unlucky in working

At the current point in time, autism spectrum conditions are still not widely understood by the public. Many people have not come into contact with a range of people on the autism spectrum and may hold media stereotypes, believing that everybody on the autism spectrum is like Dustin Hoffman's *Rain Man*. Other people may simply come from backgrounds or cultures where difference is not seen as desirable or tolerated. This means that often you have to be the ones to educate people about neurodiversity (differences in how people's brains function) and tolerance. This often starts simply by modelling and promoting attitudes you wish to see in others, and being open and honest about some of your differences. People often will not understand unless you tell them. Perhaps also there will be specific times or places when you can raise awareness in more formal ways.

Other options

Your job should be enjoyable and bring you a sense of purpose and meaning. It is not always possible to find the perfect job straight away and often our work preferences and interests change as we become older. Some people spend their whole life in the same role, others like to move up the career ladder and gain promotion, and others may change careers frequently to follow their current interests. There is no 'right' way of doing things and the employment landscape is changing a lot in the early 21st century. Here are just some of the things you may wish to consider:

Flexi-working: Some employers offer flexible working hours, so it may be possible to begin earlier or later, or to do some longer days in order to have other time in the week off.

Home-working: Depending on your job you may be able to do some of your work from home.

Part-time / Job-sharing: Working part-time or job-sharing with another person is becoming more common.

Self-employment: Setting up your own business or company is a possibility and can suit people who are well-motivated and like to work independently.

Freelancing: Being a freelancer also suits some people who prefer to work on shorter projects for different employers or organisations. Again, this is another option which allows you more control over your work-life balance.

Portfolio career: A portfolio career simply means doing two or more different things. So perhaps you work part-time for an employer but are self-employed the rest of the time.

Activity

It can be helpful to consider your life as a whole, and not just your job. Consider what sort of lifestyle you would like to lead and what your values are. See if that helps you to identify what you need and want from your job.

Things you wanted to be
when you grew up...

Your dream holiday...

Scribble Page...

An unforgettable day...

Your ideal weekend...

Lifestyle

Section 6: Lifestyle

This section is about skills needed to live independently, to stay safe, and to create the lifestyle that suits you best.

Lifestyle

Before considering some of the more practical issues, let's begin by thinking first about your lifestyle and what is important to you. You considered your values in section 1 of this book. Take a look back in your journal to what you wrote. Identifying your values can help you to set and prioritise goals that are meaningful to you.

Activity

Think about your ideal lifestyle. What would it include? You could write, draw, make a collage or create a spider diagram. Consider the following aspects, or add some of your own. What is important to you in each area?

Home Life (*where you live, who you live with, pets, cooking, gardening, activities at home...*)

Relationships (*family, relatives, friends, intimate relationships, children, acquaintances...*)

Professional Life (*job /career, opportunities for promotion, work-life balance, opportunities for professional development or further study, financial stability, making a difference ...*)

Health and Wellbeing (*physical health and fitness, mental wellbeing, opportunities for relaxation ...*)

Hobbies and Interests (*hobbies, interests, sports, membership of groups or clubs, making a living from a hobby, travel, reading, having fun / enjoyment ...*)

Community and Contribution (*volunteer or community work, involvement in the community, helping others, being part of things, causes you are passionate about, raising awareness...*)

Learning and Studying *(formal learning opportunities, work-related learning, further study, informal learning, online learning, learning new skills, teaching others…)*

Imagining your 'ideal' lifestyle can help you to identify and prioritise goals that are important to you. It can also help you to identify and appreciate what is already going well in your life.

Activity

For each heading in the last activity, give yourself a score from 1 - 10 with how satisfied you are with that aspect of your lifestyle. Think about all the positives you already experience. Next consider one or two areas you would like to improve. Identify one thing you could do to move that score up one point.

Example: *You might have identified your ideal home life would be living somewhere quiet where you feel safe. You would have friendly neighbours. Your home would be warm and comfortable, a place where you enjoy coming home to and relaxing. You would have a pet rabbit. You would have a calming décor and display some things that are meaningful to you. You would grow some vegetables and colourful flowers in pots..*

You might have given yourself 5 out of 10 for this area currently as you already live in a quiet street, feel safe and have friendly neighbours. However, your flat does not yet feel comfortable, you are not allowed pets and you have no outdoor space. So, to move to 6 or 7 out of 10, you might identify that you could do things such as grow some herbs on the windowsill, have a vase of cut flowers, and perhaps put up some posters or photographs, or buy some colourful cushions or throws to make your living space feel more comfortable.

Goal Setting and Problem Solving

Identifying goals be easier than working towards them! Often a good starting point is simply to be organised and make a to-do list. Prioritise the things important to you and write reminders of what you need to do in your diary, on your calendar or set an alarm. There are also apps available (such as 'Regularly' and 'Trello') which can help with personal organisation.

The next two pages contain goal setting and problem solving templates which could help you to organise your thoughts.

Goal Setting

What I want to achieve:		Deadline:
Steps I need to take:	Deadline:	Tick when done:
1.		
2.		
3.		
4.		
5.		

Problem Solving

The problem / issue is:		
My options:	**Pros:**	**Cons:**
Difficulties I may face in my chosen option and how I will overcome them:		

Independent Living

The rest of this section considers some practical advice for staying safe and living independently.

Wellbeing and safety in the home

Feeling safe and comfortable in the home can help to reduce anxiety levels. Some general tips include:

- Turn off electrical appliances when you have finished with them and do not leave equipment such as hair straighteners unattended
- Do not leave mobile phones or other devices charging overnight; this can be dangerous
- Mop up spills straight away to avoid slipping
- Lock doors and windows when you go out and leave valuables out of sight
- Keep your belongings tidy to help to avoid accidents such as trips and falls. This also makes it easier to find things!
- Keep your space clean to prevent infestations and illnesses
- Do not allow strangers to enter your home. If somebody is due to visit your home and you do not feel comfortable, ask a friend, relative or mentor to be there with you
- If you are sharing a house or living in halls of residence, keep your room secure and only allow in people you feel comfortable with
- Ensure that you have a smoke alarm and test it frequently to check that the batteries still work
- Do not use appliances with frayed cords or power cables as these can be dangerous
- Get things fixed or repaired as soon as possible so that they do not become worse

- Ensure you know what to do in case of a power cut or other emergency; keep a list of useful phone numbers handy

A pleasant living space can make a difference to your health and wellbeing. Keeping your house, flat or room tidy can help to reduce anxiety, and personalising your space with posters, photos and familiar objects can help to promote a feeling of wellbeing. If you have some freedom over your surroundings you might also consider re-decorating or painting so that your home reflects your tastes.

Interesting Fact

Evidence suggests that having plants and flowers indoors can benefit our health and wellbeing.[xxvii] Plants help reduce stress, and help to clean the air we breathe. They are also a relatively cheap way of adding colour and interest to our surroundings. Just make sure you remember to water them.

Safety when out and about

It is also important to consider safety and wellbeing when outside of the home. Some general tips include:

- Do not carry valuables with you when you do not need to
- If you are carrying valuables, keep them secure and do not leave your bag out of sight or where somebody could take it
- If your credit or debit cards are stolen, report it to your bank immediately and cancel the cards
- Take particular care that nobody is watching when taking money from cash machines
- When alone, stick to well-lit areas in the dark
- When using public transport in the dark, sit in well-lit carriages with other people
- Consider carrying a personal alarm

145

- If you drive, park your car in a well-lit area and do not leave valuables on display
- Plan journeys (whether by foot, bicycle, car or public transport) in advance to reduce the likelihood that you will get lost or anxious
- Do not accept lifts from strangers
- In busy clubs and pubs do not leave drinks out of sight or where they can be tampered with

These are just some basic guidelines to keep you and your possessions safe when out in public. Most of the time, you will be perfectly safe, but it is helpful to be prepared and know what to do if you do find yourself in some sort of danger. Unfortunately, not everybody we meet can be trusted; be wary of strangers who approach you and be aware that not everybody's intentions may be completely trustworthy. Tell your friends, partner or housemates where you are going and what time to expect you back. Phone or text them if your plans change.

In general, try to avoid putting yourself in a position of danger or vulnerability. Criminals, muggers and other predators often choose victims who look vulnerable and lacking in confidence. Simple measures you can take include walking tall and purposefully, and practising assertiveness techniques.

Further Information

The Crime Stoppers website contains information about keeping yourself, your possessions and your property safe, as well as information about how to report crimes (https://crimestoppers-uk.org).

If you are at university, your student support services will have information about keeping yourself safe, and any specific dangers in your area. The Complete University Guide has general safety advice for students (www.thecompleteuniversityguide.co.uk).

Life online

Much of 21st century life is spent online. Indeed, only a few years ago, some of the things we now take for granted belonged in the realms of science fiction. Just think about everything we do online: shopping; banking; booking holiday and trips; communicating with others; using social media; research; surveys; sharing photos and videos; finding information; responding to videos and articles; making complaints and enquiries; making appointments …. the list could go on and on! While the internet has certainly made life easier, it also brings dangers; it is important to be aware of these. By sharing so much of our lives online, it is becoming easier for people to commit 'identity theft', to steal our bank details and for strangers to get to know us. How can we keep ourselves safe?

- Secure your devices with a PIN code or password. Do not give this information to anybody else
- Use anti-virus software on your devices to keep them free from viruses
- Make your passwords and log-in details for various sites difficult to guess; do not give this information to anybody
- Do not pass your credit or debit card details on to others
- Buy only from reputable websites and organisations. Check a website is secure by looking for the padlock symbol in front of the web address in your browser
- Beware of websites that ask you to fill in lots of personal details as this information can then be passed on to others. Read the small print carefully. There are often tick boxes which ask you if you give your permission for your details to be shared. Read the wording carefully so that you understand what you are agreeing to

- Beware of emails which tell you that you have won prizes or which ask for money; these are usually scams designed to get money from you. Ignore them, delete and block
- Do not respond to e-mails asking for your bank details; some of these may be fake. Contact your bank directly to check if you are unsure
- Remember there is lots of 'wrong' information available on the internet; don't believe everything that you read. Check who has written the site to see if it reliable

A further danger online is the possibility of seeing inappropriate content. Many videos, games or other material have age restrictions due to the violence, language or content. Even if you are over 18, there can still be material available online which is illegal, dangerous, or which you just do not wish to access. This can include things such as pornography, child abuse images and websites which promote issues such as self-harm, eating disorders or race hate.

It can be easy on some websites to build up debts and spend more money than you intend to. Some people become addicted to online gambling or apps which require buying further levels. You might find you quickly run up a big bill without realising.

And, although it is not a pleasant topic to consider, the internet is often used for grooming and sexual abuse. Grooming is when somebody builds an emotional connection with a young person to gain their trust for the purposes of sexual exploitation or abuse.

The internet is not bad in itself, it just has to be used wisely and it is important to be aware of the dangers.

Social Media

A huge part of life online is social media. Social media includes sites such as Facebook, Twitter, Snapchat, Pinterest, Instagram, YouTube and others.

Social media has changed the way we communicate. There are many positives: we can share videos and photos instantaneously with large groups; keep in touch with friends and family living in different places; communicate with people from around the world; keep up to date with the latest news and events; and can share information with large audiences.

But social media also creates a number of challenges and difficulties:

- Information posted can be seen by everybody
- Information stays online for a long time; it is often impossible to delete completely information
- Information can be quickly passed on, shared by others, altered, changed and downloaded
- It can be easy for strangers to set up 'fake' profiles and get to know people
- It is easy for people to bully online; cyberbullying is a major cause of distress for many young people
- 'Sexting' is when people are encouraged to send sexually explicit photos of themselves to others; these can then be easily shared and is another form of bullying
- Rumours and gossip can spread quickly
- Short comments and instant messages can be easily misinterpreted as they often lack context, background and other useful information such as tone of voice and expression
- Images can be digitally manipulated
- Some people feel pressure to be constantly online, leading to stress, unhappiness and lack of sleep
- It can be easy to 'over-share' personal information which others later use to manipulate you and make you feel worse
- Exposure to constant advertising and media images can create unhappiness and make viewers compare themselves negatively to others

- It can be depressing to see constant images of others enjoying themselves and displaying their 'perfect lives'

In fact, lots of people feel overwhelmed by social media at times. It is fine to choose not to use social networks if you do not want to. It is also fine just to use one or two sites, or to log in just once a day, or once every few days rather than get constant notifications on your phone. You can change your settings on most sites to choose how often you would like to receive e-mails and notifications, and what you would like to be notified of. Choose what suits you best.

Activity

Have an online 'clear up'. List your online accounts and social networking sites. Consider:

Deleting accounts you no longer use

Changing passwords to ones that are harder to guess

Removing your details and personal information from sites you signed up to but are no longer active on

Deleting people you do not know in real life from your online networks

Deleting photos or videos you do not want shared in the future

Ensuring personal details such as your date of birth and address are not visible

Using social media wisely

As well as the above, several other things can ensure you use social media more wisely:

- Remember everything you post can be shared quickly. Do not comment on something if you are uncomfortable with it or feel it could be considered offensive or

150

cyberbullying. Avoid getting involved in online arguments or conflict

- If you do witness cyberbullying report it to the most suitable person or organisation (see below)
- Alter privacy settings so that only good friends can see items you post
- Think carefully before posting personal photos or videos. Are you happy for anybody to see this?
- Future employers will also be able to see the things that you have posted. Avoid posting anything offensive or derogatory
- Interact only with people who you know in real-life; ignore invitations and requests from strangers
- Be aware that predators often look to find victims who are vulnerable and feeling low. Avoid sharing your thoughts and feelings with strangers online as well as personal information or details
- Switch off or avoid sites which use GPS or location tagging to show where you are. This makes it easier for people to discover where you study, live, work and socialise
- Be aware most people have an 'online profile' and will only post photos and information that puts them in the best possible light. Try not to believe everything that you see or read – many people post only the 'edited highlights'
- Try not to take other people's comments too seriously. Often it is impossible to understand what people really mean when you do not have additional information such as context, tone of voice and facial expression. If you feel you might have misunderstood, try not to respond immediately in a negative way. Ask them face to face what they meant.

Life Management

Let's look now at organising and managing your personal and home life. People often spend a lot of time thinking about studying or employment but do not put the same effort into planning the rest of their life; this can sometimes lead to everyday issues becoming overwhelming. This section considers what you can do to make life at home and managing your personal finances easier.

With regards to home life and organising personal matters there are some particular difficulties some individuals on the autism spectrum might face:

- Lacking a supportive friendship group to help with everyday matters

- Being unaware of support available, or of local events, because of not being part of a friendship group or community
- Differences communicating with others
- Not wanting to ask for help
- Preferring to do things independently or alone; choosing to live alone can mean nobody to share the workload with
- Interpreting others' motives and intentions differently
- Difficulties with 'executive function' (the planning and organising of tasks)
- Having special interests which take up a lot of time
- Financial limitations, possibly due to difficulties with finding or maintaining employment
- Experiencing depression, anxiety or worry which can make everyday tasks harder to cope with
- Feeling exhausted after social interaction or experiencing sensory meltdowns / shutdowns, which can mean everyday tasks are delayed

What's important is to become aware of anything which affects you as an individual. Once you have identified these, it is easier to decide on your next steps and consider what you could do to support yourself.

Activity

Look at the list above and identify if any issues affect you. Do you find any of these things difficult to cope with at times: personal organisation, household chores, keeping your living space in a good state of repair, cooking, managing money, dealing with bills, personal hygiene, looking after pets, keeping up with phone calls and emails, getting out to events?

Note in your journal any barriers you experience to doing some of these things. Has anything worked well in the past? What other strategies could you try?

Household Chores

Whether living alone, in a shared house, in halls of residence or with your family, there are likely to be a number of household chores that are your responsibility. These often are not particularly enjoyable tasks but need to be kept on top of to ensure that your living space remains clean, hygienic and free from infestations. Some things you might need to do are:

Vacuuming	Washing dishes
Washing clothes	Ironing clothes
Cleaning the kitchen	Cleaning the bathroom
Dusting	Taking out the rubbish
Recycling	Cleaning floors
Cleaning windows	Keeping garden tidy

Sometimes household chores can seem overwhelming but in fact most are quite quick to do. It can help to keep a calendar, chart or to-do list in a visible place. Mark on the things that need to be done at a set time (e.g. taking your recycling and bins out on a set day each week). For the rest, some people prefer to set aside a time each week to complete these household tasks such as your washing and vacuuming; others prefer to do things as they need doing. Prioritise important things, such as keeping your food preparation area clean. Other chores can be done less frequently.

Cooking

Living independently, you will have to prepare your own meals. Sometimes this can cause challenges for some individuals on the autism spectrum: sensory sensitivities may mean there are foods you do not like to touch, smell or taste; motor difficulties might mean that you find the physical process of cooking difficult; you might worry about eating a balanced and healthy diet; you might find it difficult to plan meals in advance; or cooking might simply be something you are not particularly interested in or have never really learned how to do properly.

Luckily there are many different cook books and websites available for different needs: cooking on a budget; for different dietary requirements; super-quick meals to make; and easy meals to make. Take a look and learn some basic cooking skills; cooking and baking can be very enjoyable activities and there is a certain sense of accomplishment of cooking a meal from scratch.

Further Information

Easy recipe ideas can be found on websites such as the BBC Good Food Website (www.bbcgoodfood.co.uk) and Student Recipes (https://studentrecipes.com).

Housing Difficulties

At times you might have to find appropriate housing, move home or negotiate difficulties with your landlord.

Activity

Consider your housing needs. Would you consider sharing a house with others? If so, what might be some difficulties you could face? What else is important to you when it comes to housing? Do you have any sensory needs you need to consider?

There are different options when it comes to where to live:

Living with parents / family: This may suit some people, but others prefer to live independently or need to move to a different area for work or study.

Living in halls of residence / student accommodation: These are usually provided for first year university students and some older students. Check with your university what is available and what the costs are. Bills (except for television licences and phone calls) are usually included in the fees.

Sharing a house with friends / doing a house- or flat- share: This is common for younger adults. Individuals usually have their own room; communal areas such as bathrooms and kitchens are shared. Everybody will pay a set amount of rent; this is usually cheaper than renting a property alone. Bills are usually shared.

Private renting: You rent a house or flat from a private landlord. You usually pay a monthly rent and bills.

Council housing / social housing / housing associations: The housing under these schemes are usually offered to people on a low income or who need extra support. The offer will vary depending on your local council. You will often be put on a waiting list for these properties. Again, you will pay rent and bills.

Buying a house / flat: To buy your own house or flat you will need to save up a deposit and then apply for a mortgage (bank loan) which you pay back monthly. You will also need to pay your bills.

Further Information

Housing options available vary from area to area. Issues regarding housing which are likely to be individual to your particular situation. The following websites can be good sources of information:

The Gov.uk website has an easy to read section about housing (www.gov.uk).

The Citizens Advice Bureau (CAB) has an informative website about housing issues such as finding somewhere to live, mortgage and rent problems, landlord disputes and housing problems (www.citizensadvice.org.uk).

If you are a student, your university will have an accommodation service which can signpost you to suitable housing and accommodation.

Managing Money

Money problems can be commonplace; many people find they do not have enough money to cover their bills or do not manage their money effectively. Budgeting is a skill worth mastering as money difficulties can cause worry and stress. Being in debt and owing money can also cause bigger problems.

Budgeting

First consider the financial expenses that you have. These are your outgoings and might include:

- Mortgage payments or rent
- Council tax
- Utility bills such as water, gas and electric
- Television licence
- Broadband / line rental
- Mobile phone contract / top up
- Car insurance
- Home insurance
- Petrol
- Public transport costs
- Pension contributions
- Student loan repayments
- Other loan repayments
- Food
- Household items
- Toiletries
- Hobbies and sports activities
- Memberships
- Socialising
- Clothes
- Buying books, newspapers, magazines and other personal items
- Pet expenses
- Health Care (e.g. dental appointments, medications)

Some general tips for managing money:

- Pay bills as soon as you can so they do not begin to mount up; look to see what the cheapest option is. Sometimes you may have to pay extra to pay monthly rather than annually, for example.
- Consider contracts very carefully before you sign up; many commit you for a year or more and you may have to pay a fee if you want to leave early
- Pay-as-you-go and pre-payment cards can help you keep track of spending on mobile phones and other utilities
- Set up direct debits or standing orders for regular payments so that you do not forget to pay these
- Shop around for the cheapest option for products and services. Look for cheaper options when it comes to renewing policies
- Be wary of salespeople who try to sell you extra products or services which you might not need
- Check bank statements regularly to ensure you are not paying for anything you did not realise you were
- Be assertive with people who cold-call or try to sell you things that you do not want. Say simply, 'No, *thank you. I'm not interested.*'
- Set yourself a weekly budget and try to stick to it
- Use some of the websites below for ideas on how to shop wisely and save money

- If you are seeking work, or on a low income, you might be entitled to benefits to help you cover costs. These include housing benefit, jobseekers allowance, or universal credit. What you are entitled to depends on your age and circumstances

This book cannot cover in detail all of the issues relating to managing money. The aim is simply to help you become more aware of your particular needs and places that you can look to get further support. Some of the most useful are listed in the box below.

Further Information

The National Autistic Society (NAS) has a free online module about managing money aimed at people on the autism spectrum. This is available at www.autismtrainingonline.com. There is also more information about budgeting, benefits and managing finances on the NAS website (www.autism.org.uk).

The Citizens Advice Bureau again has very useful sections on money-related issues and benefits, as does the Gov.uk website.

A useful website which contains tips and strategies on how to save money is Money Saving Expert (www.moneysavingexpert.com).

When dealing with issues such as housing, bills, money and benefits, there can be a lot of jargon used and paperwork to fill in. Keep any paperwork you are sent and make copies of forms you fill in. Keep a folder with file dividers or a computer file to hold all of your documents relating to different topics. There are people who can help you with these issues: autism organisations and charities; student support services; mentors; and other charities and voluntary organisations. Sometimes it can help to take a friend or relative to appointments with you.

Dealing with these things often means you need to interact with a range of people in different services and organisations, either face-to-face or by phone. Sometimes this type of communication can be difficult for some individuals on the autism spectrum. Having worked through this book you should now be more aware of how you can develop skills of communication and assertiveness. You will have become more aware of the differences and difficulties your autism may cause. Being able to identify these can help enormously as you will feel more confident about communicating your needs to different professionals and making them aware of how autism affects you.

General tips:

- Tell your mentors or advisors about your autism and how it affects you as an individual; remember that nor everybody has a good understanding of autism so they might not be aware of some of the differences or difficulties you experience
- Do not be afraid to ask people to explain things again or to explain things differently if you have not understood
- Take a friend or relative along to meetings if it helps you
- Ask how you are best to get in touch with your mentor or advisor. Take a note of their e-mail, phone number or booking system
- Ask for written information if you process this better and so that you can read it in your own time
- Take notes in meetings so that you do not forget what is being said

---

Activity

Set aside a time to organise your paperwork and important documents. This will help you to feel organised and be able to find information more easily. Try sorting into categories such as: certificates; important documents; housing; banking; receipts; bills; mobile phone; study-related; work-related.

Looking after pets

For many people, life would not be the same without a pet. They can bring pleasure, joy and companionship. Dog owners often identify taking their pet out for regular walks helps their own fitness and wellbeing levels, as well as being a good way of meeting other people.

Interesting Fact

Several studies suggest animals can be particularly beneficial for individuals on the autism spectrum. In addition, some individuals on the autism spectrum find that they connect with animals more easily than with people. If this applies to you, it may be worth considering owning a pet, helping others look after pets, or working / volunteering with animals.

If considering sharing your life with a pet, you will have to take into consideration:

- The financial cost of buying the pet and also pet food, toys, bedding, other equipment, annual vet fees and insurance
- Whether you have the physical space for a pet to live, and an outdoor area for animals such as cats, dogs, horses or chickens
- The daily commitment: some animals such as dogs need human companionship and daily walks
- Who will look after the pet when you go away on holiday, or is there a pet sitting service / kennels / cattery to use
- Young kittens and puppies require training
- Rescue animals might have been mistreated so can be wary around humans or other animals
- The lifestyle changes: pets require play time and training, many will make a mess around the house at first and some are likely to cause destruction until they are fully trained. Are you prepared for the cleaning up and mess?

Think about these things carefully if you are considering getting a pet. It is a big decision, but one that can be very rewarding.

Further Information

If you are researching pet ownership, some good websites to start with are the PDSA (www.pdsa.org.uk) and the RSPCA (www.rspca.org.uk).

Final Thoughts

You are now coming to the end of this book. You have considered in greater detail how your autism affects different aspects of your life. You have reflected on what makes you an individual and what is important to you. You have also considered some practical skills and advice that will enable you to succeed in studying, employment and living independently.

Activity

What are your thoughts about your autism now? How does it affect you? What are the positive and negative aspects of it?

You will realise by now that autism is simply a different way of being from the majority. It need not be considered a disease, disorder or disability. Hopefully this book has helped you to identify why some difficulties or differences have come about. Often, it is simply because the world is currently geared towards a non-autistic way of thinking and being.

Activity

Which strategies or ideas from this book are you going to continue to put into practice? Are there any you will try at a later date, or you will adapt for the future?

Throughout this book various strategies and ideas have been suggested to help you understand yourself and to support you in creating a life that is meaningful to you. Perhaps you have found some of these activities useful, or adapted them to make them work for you. Over time you will develop your own way of doing things.

Perhaps you have also realised that your attitude to your autism can make all of the difference. If you decide that your autism is going to be a problem, then it will be. If you decide that you are not going to let your autism define you, then it won't do! Developing confidence and self-esteem can be hugely beneficial. Approach your autism with curiosity, acceptance and confidence.

Activity

What advice would you give to your younger self, or to other young people on the autism spectrum?

Your autism does not stop here; it is something you continue to learn about throughout your life. Learning about yourself accepting who you are can be both challenging and hugely liberating. It is a journey worth pursuing. Your relationship with yourself is one that will be lifelong.

Although learning about your autism is important and helps you to make sense of how you interact with the world, you are more than your autism. Do not let 'having autism' become an excuse; it should not prevent you from working towards your goals, taking on challenges, or enjoying life. Celebrate the fact that you are a true individual with unique strengths and skills. In an ideal world, perhaps labels such as 'Asperger's' or 'autism' would not even be necessary at all; diversity of all kinds would simply be accepted and expected!

Your comfiest clothing…

A household chore that
makes you feel
accomplished…

Scribble Page…

Your favourite meals and
snacks…

Your favourite scents…

References

Section 1: Self
[i] Keeping a journal has been shown to increase happiness and support emotional regulation: Roberts M (2015) 'Write your thoughts in a diary', Psychologies Magazine, August 2015, p39

[ii] Writing our life story can help us to make sense of what has happened to us: Regan K (2015) 'Let me tell you a story', Psychologies Magazine, November 2015, p64-9

[iii] For more information on the idea of 'flow' research the psychologist Mihaly Csikszentmihalyi who first identified the state.

[iv] A recent book which investigates the history of autism spectrum conditions is 'Neurotribes' by Steve Silberman.

[v] For more information about Asperger syndrome, see 'The Complete Guide to Asperger Syndrome' by Tony Attwood.

[vi] Using our strengths is considered to be one of the most direct routes to personal fulfilment: Boniwell I (2008) Positive Psychology in a Nutshell, Open University Press, London. Using our core strengths also means we are likely to feel more confident, less stressed and more likely to achieve our goals: King V (2015), 'Why goals make us happy', Psychologies, August 2015, p60.

[vii] Simone R (2010) Aspergirls: Empowering females with Asperger Syndrome, Jessica Kingsley Publishers, London

[viii] Jamison TR & Schuttler JO (2015) 'Examining social competence, self-perception, quality of life and internalising and externalising symptoms in adolescent females with and without autism spectrum disorder', Molecular Autism, September 2015, 17, p6-53

Section 2: Health & Well-being
[ix] National Health Service (NHS) (2013) 'Why lack of sleep is bad for your health', online, www.nhs.uk/livewell/tiredness-and-fatigue/pages/lack-of-sleep-health-risks.aspx (accessed June 2015)

[x] NAS (2016) 'Sex Education and Puberty', online, http://www.autism.org.uk/about/communication/sex-education.aspx (accessed October 2016)

[xi] Many studies in which participants have been asked to 'count their blessings' have been shown to improve happiness: Carr A (2011) Positive Psychology: The science of happiness and human strengths, Routledge, London.

[xii] There is evidence which suggests those on the autism spectrum may be more likely to experience mental health difficulties such as depression, anxiety and obsessive-compulsive disorder: Kim et al (2000) 'The prevalence of anxiety and mood problems among children with autism

and Asperger syndrome, Autism: The International Journal of Research and Practice, 4 (2), p117-32

[xiii] More information about resilience can be found in Cyrulnik B (2009) Resilience: How your inner strength can set you free from the past, Penguin, London.

[xiv] Peter Vermeulen, a researcher at Autisme Centraal has written a number of papers on autism and wellbeing. He discusses the importance of not making somebody less autistic, but on making them more 'autistically happy'.

Section 3: Friendships, relationships and communication

[xv] For more information on some of the communication differences often associated with autism spectrum conditions, visit the National Autistic Society website, or read Tony Attwood's 'The Complete Guide to Asperger Syndrome'.

[xvi] Peter Vermeulen's book, 'Autism as Context Blindness' (2009) suggests that 'context' is what creates difficulties for those on the autism spectrum.

[xvii] Goman CK (2011) 'Seven Seconds to Make a First Impression', Forbes.com, online, (accessed October 2016) http://www.forbes.com/sites/carolkinseygoman/2011/02/13/seven-seconds-to-make-a-first-impression/2/#57f5e4777e6a

[xviii] Many articles and books have been written about differences in male and female conversation styles. These can give some insight into some of the difficulties and differences women on the autism spectrum may experience in comparison to their male counterparts. Autism researcher, Simon Baron-Cohen, devised the 'extreme male brain' theory relating to autism which suggests that autism may be an extreme form of the 'systemising' brain rather than the 'empathising' brain.

[xix] Simone R (2010) Aspergirls: empowering females with Asperger Syndrome, Jessica Kingsley Publishers, London.

[xx] Hurley E (2014) Ultraviolet Voices: Stories of women on the autism spectrum, Autism West Midlands, Birmingham, UK

[xxi] If you are an introvert and want to know more about this, try reading Susan Cain's 'Quiet: the power of introverts in a world that can't stop talking' (2012).

[xxii] Attwood T (2008) The Complete Guide to Asperger Syndrome, Jessica Kingsley Publishers, London.

[xxiii] Simon Baron-Cohen has written about empathy in relation to autism. One of his most popular books is 'Zero degrees of empathy' (2012).

[xxiv] Kidd & Castano (2013) 'Reading literary fiction improves theory of mind', Science, 18 October 2013, 342 (6156), p377-80

Section 4: Learning

[xxv] These templates and other information in this chapter has been adapted from Honeybourne V (2016) Educating and supporting girls with Asperger's and autism: a resource for education and health professionals, Speechmark, London

Section 5: Employment

[xxvi] Information in this chapter has been adapted from Honeybourne V (2016) Educating and supporting girls with Asperger's and autism: a resource for education and health professionals, Speechmark, London

Section 6: Life Skills

[xxvii] The relative benefits of green versus lean office space: Three field experiments. Nieuwenhuis, Marlon; Knight, Craig; Postmes, Tom; Haslam, S. Alexander Journal of Experimental Psychology: Applied, Vol 20(3), Sep 2014, 199-214

Made in the USA
San Bernardino, CA
05 April 2019